For the Love of Bob

About the Author

James Bowen is a street musician in London. He found Bob the cat in 2007 and the pair have been inseparable ever since.

For the Love of Bob

James Bowen

HODDER

First published in Great Britain in 2014 by Hodder & Stoughton
An Hachette UK company

1

Copyright © James and Bob Ltd and Connected Content Ltd 2014

The right of James Bowen and Garry Jenkins to be identified as the
Authors of the Work has been asserted by them in accordance with the
Copyright, Designs and Patents Act 1988.

A CIP catalogue record for this title is available from the British Library

Paperback ISBN 978 1 444 79405 2
Ebook ISBN 978 1 444 79404 5

Typeset by Hewer Text UK Ltd, Edinburgh
Printed and bound by CPI Group (UK) Ltd, Croydon, CR0 4YY

Hodder & Stoughton policy is to use papers that are natural,
renewable and recyclable products and made from wood grown
in sustainable forests. The logging and manufacturing processes
are expected to conform to the environmental regulations
of the country of origin.

Hodder & Stoughton Ltd
338 Euston Road
London NW1 3BH

www.hodder.co.uk

To Garry, my mentor and teacher,
Mary, my angel from Angel and
Rowena and Kerry who took a chance
on me. I love them all greatly. Also,
special praise to my Kitty Belle, who
has become essential to Bob and me.

Contents

There is something about the presence of a cat . . . that seems to take the bite out of being alone.

Louis Camuti

If man could be crossed with the cat, it would improve man but deteriorate the cat.

Mark Twain

Chapter 1
A Bad Start

Our bad day began when my alarm
failed to go off. I'd overslept.

'Bob!' I gasped. 'We're going to be
late!'

Bob looked at me with his big green
eyes.

Chill out, James, he seemed to say. *We
have this under control.*

I wrapped an extra-thick scarf around

Bob's neck to keep out the chill then I grabbed my stuff. We dashed out of my flat in Tottenham, north London, heading for the bus that would take us to Islington, where I sold the homeless magazine *The Big Issue*. Bob ran beside me. We leaped on to the bus with moments to spare.

'We made it!' I said in relief.

But barely five minutes into our journey, things went from bad to worse.

Bob was in his usual position, half asleep on the seat next to me, when he suddenly lifted his head, looking around suspiciously.

I smell trouble, his body language said.

In the two years since I'd met him, Bob was usually right. Today was no exception. Within moments the bus was filled with an acrid, burning smell.

'This journey is terminating here,' said the panicked driver over the speaker. 'Everyone off the bus. Immediately!'

It wasn't quite the evacuation of the *Titanic*, but the bus was three quarters full so there was a lot of chaotic pushing and jostling. Bob didn't seem in a rush. Deciding to trust him, I left the others to it. So Bob and I were among the last to get off. As it turned out, that was a wise decision. The bus may have smelled awful but at least it was warm.

We had stopped opposite a new building site. Icy winds were whipping towards us through the site at a rate of knots. I was glad that I'd wrapped the extra-thick, woollen scarf around Bob's neck that morning.

'It's just an overheated engine,' the driver informed us after a few minutes.

'We have to wait for a bus company mechanic to fix it.'

So, amid much grumbling and complaining, about two dozen of us were left standing on the freezing cold pavement for almost half an hour while we waited for a replacement bus.

By the time Bob and I hopped off at our destination, Islington Green, we had been on the road for more than an hour and a half. We were now seriously late. I was going to miss the lunchtime rush, one of the best times for selling the magazine.

As usual, the five-minute walk to Angel tube station was a stop-start affair. It always was when I had Bob with me. Sometimes I walked with him on a leather lead, but more often than not he perched on my shoulders, gazing curiously out at the world, like the look-out on the prow of a ship. It wasn't something people were used to seeing every day of the week, so we could never walk more than ten yards without someone wanting to say hello and stroke him, or take a photograph. That didn't bother me at all. I knew Bob relished the attention.

The first person to stop us today was a little Russian lady.

'Oh, *koschka*, so pretty!' she said.

I stopped to let her say hello properly, but she immediately reached up to Bob and tried to touch him on the nose. Not a clever move.

Bob lashed out with a wild wave of his paw and a very loud *eeeeeow*. Fortunately he didn't scratch the lady, but he did leave her a little shaken. I had to spend a few minutes making sure she was all right.

'You should never do that to an animal, madam,' I told her, smiling and being as polite as possible. 'How would you react if someone tried to put their hands on your face? You're lucky he didn't scratch you.'

'I no mean to upset him,' she said. 'I very sorry, very sorry.'

I felt a bit sorry for her.

'Come on, you two, let's be friends,' I said.

Bob eventually allowed her to run her hand, very gently, along the back of his neck. The lady was very apologetic – and very hard to shake off.

When we finally got to the tube station, I put my rucksack on the pavement so that Bob could lie down on it – our regular routine. Then I started laying out my stack of *The Big Issue* magazines. I had to sell at least a couple of dozen today because, as usual, I needed the money.

But before I'd managed to sell a single magazine the heavens opened, raining down on me and Bob and forcing us to take shelter in an underpass near a bank and some office buildings.

Bob really hates the rain, especially when it's freezing cold. This day he almost seemed to shrink in it. His bright marmalade-coloured coat also seemed to turn a little bit greyer and less notice-able. Unsurprisingly, fewer people than usual stopped to make a fuss over him, so I sold fewer magazines than usual too.

Bob was soon making it clear that he didn't want to hang around. He kept shooting me withering looks and, like some kind of ginger hedgehog, scrunched himself up into a ball.

'I get the message, Bob,' I sighed. 'But it's nearly the weekend and I need to make enough money to keep us both going. My stack of magazines is still as thick as when we arrived. We have to sell some!'

Chapter 2
The Night Watchman

The weather wasn't improving. Then, midway through the afternoon, a young, uniformed police officer approached us.

'Are you supposed to be selling those magazines here, sir?' he said.

'I am perfectly entitled to sell magazines here, officer,' I said politely. 'I have my registered vendor ID and, unless I am causing a public nuisance, I can sell magazines at this spot from dawn 'til dusk.'

He looked unconvinced. 'Turn out your pockets, sir,' he said. 'Let's see what you've got.'

I had no idea what he was frisking me for but he didn't find anything.

'This cat yours, sir?' he asked, turning his attention to Bob now.

'Yes, officer,' I said. 'He is legally registered to me and microchipped.'

That seemed to worsen his mood. He walked off with a look almost as grim as the weather.

By early evening, I decided to call it quits. I felt deflated. I'd barely sold ten magazines and made only a fraction of what I'd normally expect to make. I'd spent long enough living off tins of reduced price beans and even cheaper loaves of bread to know that I wouldn't starve. I had enough money to top up the gas and electric meters and buy a meal or two for Bob as well. But it meant I'd probably need to head out to work again over the weekend. I really didn't want to do that. More rain was forecast, and I was starting to feel under the weather myself.

On the bus home, I could feel the first signs of flu seeping into my bones. I was aching and having hot flushes.

That's all I need, I thought, easing myself deep into my bus seat and settling down for a nap.

By now the sky had turned an inky black and the streetlights were on full blaze. There was something about London at night that fascinated Bob. As I drifted in and out of sleep, he sat beside me staring out of the bus window, lost in his own world.

Somewhere past Newington Green, I must have dropped off to sleep completely. I was woken by something lightly tapping me on the leg and the feeling of whiskers brushing against my cheek. I opened my eyes to see Bob with his face close to mine, patting me on the knee with his paw.

'What is it?' I said, slightly grumpily.

He started making a move off the seat towards the aisle, throwing me slightly concerned glances as he did so.

Are you coming or not? he seemed to say.

I looked out on to the street and realised where we were – right by where we needed to get off! Grabbing my rucksack, I hit the stop button just in the nick of time. If it hadn't been for my little night watchman, we'd have flown past our bus stop.

On the way home I popped into the convenience store on the corner of our road and bought myself some cheap flu remedy tablets. I also got Bob some nibbles and a pouch of his favourite chicken dinner. It was the least I could do. It had been a miserable day and it would have been easy to feel sorry for myself. But, back in the warmth of my little, one-bedroomed flat, I realised something.

'I have no real cause to complain, do I, Bob?' I said, watching him wolfing down his food. 'If I'd stayed asleep on the bus much longer I could easily have ended up miles away.'

Looking out of the window, I could see that the weather was getting worse. If I'd been out in this rain, I could easily have developed something a lot worse than mild flu. I'd had a fortunate escape.

I was lucky in more ways than one. There's an old saying I know: *A wise man doesn't grieve for the things he doesn't have, but is grateful for the good things that he does have.*

After dinner, I sat on the sofa, wrapped in a blanket and sipping a hot drink. I looked at Bob snoozing contentedly in his favourite spot near the radiator. To him, our earlier troubles were long forgotten. In that moment he couldn't have been happier.

'I should view the world the same way,' I told myself. After all, there were so many good things I was grateful for at this moment in my life. Not least of them, Bob himself.

It was now a little over two years since I had found Bob, lying injured on the ground floor of this same block of flats. When I spotted him in the dingy light of the hallway, he looked like he'd been attacked by another animal. He had wounds on the back of his legs and on his body.

At first I thought he belonged to someone else. But after seeing him in the same place for a few days, I took him up to my flat and nursed him back to health. I had to fork out almost every penny I had to buy him medicine, but it was worth it. We formed an instant bond.

Bob appeared to be a stray so I assumed that he'd return to the streets. But he refused to leave my side. Each day I'd put him outside and try to send him on his way, and each day he'd follow

me down the road or pop up in the hallway in the evening, inviting himself in
for the night.

They say that cats choose you, not the
other way round. I realised Bob had
chosen me when he followed me to the
bus stop a mile from home. When I
shooed him away and watched him disappear into the busy crowds, I thought
that was the last I'd see of him. But as
the bus was pulling away, Bob appeared
out of nowhere, leaping on board in a
blur of ginger, plonking himself down on
the seat next to me. And that had been
that.

Bob and I were kindred spirits,
helping each other to heal the wounds
of our troubled pasts. I gave Bob com-
panionship, food and somewhere warm
to lay his head at night. In return he

gave me a new hope and purpose in life. He gave me loyalty, love and humour, and a sense of responsibility I'd never felt before. He also gave me some goals and helped me see the world more clearly than I had done for a long, long time.

For more than a decade I'd been a drug addict, sleeping rough around London, oblivious to the world around me.

As a homeless person, I was invisible. I forgot how to function and how to interact with people. In a way I was dead to the world. But now, with Bob's help, I was slowly coming back to life. I was still on medication, but could see the light at the end of the tunnel. I hoped to be completely drug-free soon.

It wasn't easy. It never is for a recovering addict. Working on the streets didn't help. Trouble was always around the corner, and I had a knack for attracting it. I longed to get off the streets and put that life behind me. I had no idea when or how that was going to be possible but, with Bob beside me, I was determined to try.

By most people's standards, I still didn't have much. I never had a lot of money and I didn't live in a flashy apartment or have a car. But I had my flat and my job selling *The Big Issue*. For the first time in years, I was heading in the right direction – with Bob to offer me friendship and to guide me on my way.

As I picked myself up and headed to bed for an early night, I leaned over and gave Bob a gentle ruffle on the back of his neck.

'Where would I be without you, little fella?'

Chapter 3
New Tricks

Some people start their mornings listening to the radio, others with their exercises or a cup of tea or coffee. Bob and I start ours by playing games together.

The moment I wake up, Bob shuffles out of his bed in the corner of the bedroom, walks over and starts staring at me. Soon after that he starts making a chirruping noise, a bit like a phone.

Brr, brr.

If that doesn't get my full attention, he starts making another noise, slightly more plaintive and pleading.

Waaaah. Waaaah!

Sometimes he places his paws on the side of the mattress and hauls himself up so that he is almost at eye-level with me. He then dabs a paw in my direction.

Don't ignore me! he seems to say. *I've been awake for ages and I'm hungry, so where's my breakfast?*

If I am too slow to respond, he steps up the charm offensive and does what I call a 'Puss in Boots', like the character in the *Shrek* movies, and stares wide-eyed at me with his piercing green eyes. It is heartbreakingly cute and totally irresistible. It always makes me smile. And it always works.

21

I always keep a packet of Bob's favourite snacks in a drawer by the side of the bed. Depending on how I am feeling, I might let him come up on the bed for a cuddle and a couple of treats. Or, if I am in a more playful mood, I'll throw them around the room for him to chase. Bob often catches the treats in mid-flight, like a cricketer or baseball player fielding a ball. He leaps up and catches them in his paws. He has even caught them in his mouth a couple of times. It's amazing to watch.

On other occasions, he'll entertain himself. One hot summer's morning, for instance, Bob was curled up in a shady spot in the bedroom fast asleep. Or so I thought.

Suddenly he sat up and jumped on the bed. Using it as a trampoline, he bounced himself at the wall behind my head, hitting it quite hard with his paws.

'Bob, what the — ?' I said, gobsmacked.

I looked at the duvet and saw a little millipede lying there. Bob was eyeing it, clearly ready to crunch it in his mouth.

'Oh no you don't, mate,' I said, knowing that insects can be poisonous to cats. 'You don't know where that's been.'

He shot me a look. *Spoilsport*, he seemed to say.

I have always been amazed at Bob's speed, strength and athleticism. Someone suggested to me once that he must be related to a lynx or some kind of wild cat. It is entirely possible. Bob's past is a complete mystery to me. I don't know how old he is and I know nothing about the life he led before I found him. Unless I do a DNA test on him, I'll never know where he comes from or who his parents were. To be honest though, I don't really care. Bob is Bob. And that is all I need to know.

I am not the only one who's learned to love Bob for being his colourful, unpre-dictable self.

In the spring of 2009, we had been selling *The Big Issue* for a year or so, and Bob had built up a small but dedicated band of admirers at our pitch outside the Angel Islington tube station.

As far as I knew, we were the only human/feline team selling *The Big Issue* in London. But even if there was another one, I suspected the feline part of the partnership wasn't much competition for Bob when it came to drawing – and pleasing – a crowd.

During our early days together, when I had been a busker in Covent Garden playing the guitar and singing, Bob had just sat there, Buddha-like, watching the world going about its business. People were fascinated by him and would stop, stroke and talk to him.

'What's your story?' they would ask. 'How did you guys meet?'

And I'd tell them. But that was about the extent of it.

Since we'd been selling *The Big Issue*, however, we'd developed a few tricks.

Bob loved to play, so I'd bring along little toys that he would toss around and chase. His favourite was a little grey mouse that had once been filled with catnip.

The mouse had lost its catnip a long time ago. Its stitching was coming apart and, although it had always been grey, it had now become a really dirty shade of grey. Bob had loads of other toys but 'Scraggedy Mouse', as I called it, was his number one toy.

He would hold it in his mouth, flicking it from side to side. Sometimes he'd whirl it around by its tail and release it so that it flew a couple of feet away. Then he'd pounce on it and start the whole process again. Bob loved hunting real mice, so he was obviously mimicking that. It always stopped people in their tracks. I'd known commuters to spend ten minutes standing there, hypnotised by Bob and his game.

Soon I started playing too. To begin with, Bob and I just played at shaking hands. I'd stretch out my hand and Bob would extend his paw to hold it. We were only doing what we did at home in my flat but people seemed to find it sweet. If I had a pound for every time someone – usually a lady – stopped and said something like, 'Aah, how sweet!' or 'That's adorable!' I'd be rich.

My playtimes with Bob became more than simple entertainment for the passing crowds. It helped me to pass the time, to keep warm on the freezing street and to enjoy my days a little more too. It also encouraged people to buy copies of the magazine. It was another one of the blessings that Bob had bestowed on me.

We began to develop our act a little further.

Bob loved his little treats. For instance,

if I held a cat biscuit three feet or so above him, he'd stand on his hind legs in an effort to snaffle the snack from my hand. He would wrap his paws around my wrist to steady himself, then let go with one paw and try to grab it.

This went down a storm. So we developed the trick even more. Bob's grip when he grabbed my arm to reach the treat was as strong as a vice. So every now and again I would slowly and very gently raise him in the air so that he was dangling a few inches above the ground. He would hang there for a few seconds until he let go, or I eased him back to earth. I always made sure he had a soft landing of course, and usually put my rucksack under him.

The more of a show we put on, the more people seemed to respond to us.

They became more generous too and not just in buying *The Big Issue*.

Since our early days, people had been incredibly kind, giving us cat snacks and nibbles. They had also started giving us items of clothing, often hand-knitted or sewn by them. Bob now had a collection of scarves in all sorts of colours, and I was running out of space to keep them all. It was a little overwhelming at times to receive such warmth, support and love.

But those who felt very differently about us were never very far away . . .

Chapter 4
A Tough Customer

It was the Friday evening rush hour, and the crowds passing in and out of Angel tube station were growing thicker by the minute. Bob was totally oblivious to the commotion, flapping his tail absent-mindedly from side to side as he lay on my rucksack on the pavement.

I suddenly noticed a lady standing a

few feet away from us. She was staring intently at Bob.

From the way she was muttering and shaking her head, I sensed she disapproved of us. I didn't plan on talking to her, mainly because I was too busy trying to sell the last few copies of the magazine before the weekend. Unfortunately, she had other ideas.

'Young man. Can't you see that this cat is in distress?' she said, approaching us.

She looked like a headmistress: middle-aged with a cut-glass English accent and wearing a tweed skirt and jacket. But she was much more aggressive than any teacher I remember.

'I have been watching you for a while and I can see that your cat is wagging its tail,' she said. 'That means it's not happy.

You shouldn't be exploiting it like this. You aren't fit to look after it.'

We'd heard this a lot since Bob and I had started working the streets together. I politely defended myself from the lady's accusations.

'He's wagging his tail because he's content. If he didn't want to be here, madam, you wouldn't see him for dust. He's a cat. They choose who they want to be with. He's free to run off whenever he wants.'

'So why is he on a lead?' she shot back, a smug look on her face.

'He's only on a lead here and when we are on the streets,' I explained. 'He ran off once and was terrified when he couldn't find me again. I let him off when he goes to do his business. So, again, if he wasn't happy, as you claim, he'd be gone the minute I took the lead off, wouldn't he?'

This lady was having none of it.

'No, no, no. It's a well-known fact that if a cat is wagging its tail it is a distress signal,' she said, more animated now.

Bob had begun backing towards me, ready to jump into my arms if things got out of hand. I tried to ease the lady's fears by telling her a little about us.

'We've been together for more than two years. He wouldn't have been with me two minutes if I was mistreating him,' I said.

But whatever I said, she just shook her head and tutted away.

'Why don't we agree to differ?' I said at last.

'*Hffff*,' she said, waving her arms at me. 'I'm not agreeing with anything you say, young man.'

To my huge relief, she started walking

away into the crowds jostling around the entrance to the tube station.

I was soon distracted by a couple of customers. Their smiles were a welcome relief. I was handing one of them their change when I heard a noise behind me that I recognised immediately.

Wheeeeeow! Bob yowled.

I spun round. Not only had the woman in the tweed suit come back, she was now holding Bob in her arms. She held him awkwardly, one hand under his stomach and another on his back, as if she'd never picked up an animal before. She could have been holding a joint of meat that she'd just bought at the butcher.

Bob was clearly furious and was wriggling like crazy.

'What do you think you are doing?' I

shouted. 'Put him down or I'll call the police!'

'He needs to be taken somewhere safe,' she said, a slightly crazed expression on her face.

She was going to run off with him! I prepared to drop my supply of magazines and chase her through the streets of Islington.

Luckily, Bob's long lead was still tethered to my rucksack. For a moment there was a kind of stand-off. But then I saw her eye moving along the lead to the rucksack.

'No you don't,' I said, stepping forward to intercept her.

My movement caught her off guard. This gave Bob his chance.

Wheeeeow! he screeched again and freed himself from the woman's grip. He didn't scratch her, but he did dig his paws into her arm which forced her to drop him on to the pavement.

He landed with a bit of a bump, then stood there growling and hissing and baring his teeth at her. I'd never seen him so aggressive.

Unbelievably, the lady used this as an argument against me.

'See? He's angry,' she said, addressing the watching crowd.

'He's angry because you just picked him up without his permission,' I said. 'He only lets me pick him up.'

'No, he's angry because of the way you are treating him,' she insisted. 'Everyone can see that. That's why he should be taken away from you. He doesn't want to be with you.'

Everyone held their breath to see what

happened next. It was Bob who broke the silence.

He gave the woman a really disdainful look, then padded his way back towards me. He began rubbing his head against the outside of my leg, and purring noisily when I put my hand down to stroke him.

He then plonked his rear down on the ground and looked up at me playfully.

Now can we get on with some more tricks? he seemed to say.

I dipped my hand into my coat pocket and produced a treat. Almost immediately, Bob got up on his hind legs and grabbed hold of my arm. I then popped the treat into his mouth drawing a couple of audible *aaahs* from somewhere behind me.

Bob had played to the crowd perfectly. It was as if he was saying: *I'm with James, and I'm really happy to be with James. And anyone who says otherwise is mistaken. End of story.*

Most of the onlookers got the message. They turned to the woman in the tweed suit.

'We know this guy, he's cool,' one young man in a business suit said.

'Yes, leave them alone. They're not doing anyone any harm and he looks after his cat really well,' another middle-aged lady said.

One or two other people made supportive noises. Not one person backed up the lady in the tweed suit. She spluttered and grumbled for a moment or two, but realised that she had lost the battle. So she disappeared once more into the crowds, this time – thankfully – permanently.

'You OK, James?' one of the onlookers asked me, as I kneeled down to check
on Bob. He was purring loudly, but his
breathing was steady and there was no
sign of any injury from when he was
dropped to the ground.

'I'm fine, thanks,' I muttered, not
being entirely honest.

I hated it when people implied I was using Bob. It hurt me deeply. Bob wanted to be with me. He'd proven that time and time again. Unfortunately, that meant that he had to spend his days with me on the streets. Those were the simple facts of my life. I didn't have a choice.

This made us easy targets. Most people judged us kindly. I had learned to accept that there would always be those who would not.

Chapter 5
The Bobmobile

It was a balmy, early summer afternoon and I decided to stop work early. The sunny weather had put a smile on everyone's face and I'd sold out my supply of magazines in a few hours.

Before I caught the bus home, I decided to buy some more magazines for the rest of the week. With Bob on my shoulders, I headed over to see Rita, the co-ordinator for *The Big Issue*, on the north side of Islington High Street.

From a distance, I could see that she and a group of vendors in red bibs were huddled around something. It turned out to be a bicycle.

'What's this, Rita?' I joked. 'Riding in the Tour de France?'

'Don't think so, James,' she smiled. 'Someone just sold it to me in exchange for ten magazines. I don't know what to do with it.'

The bike wasn't in prime condition. There was rust on the handlebars and the light at the front had cracked glass. The paintwork had a few chips and nicks and, just for good measure, one of the mudguards had been snapped in half.

'Is it roadworthy?' I asked Rita.

'I think so,' she said. 'Apart from the front brakes needing a bit of attention.'

I stared at the bike. I was no Bradley Wiggins, but I had ridden bikes throughout my childhood and again in London. And I knew a bit about cycle maintenance.

'Why don't you give it a try?' Rita suggested, seeing the look in my eye.

'Why not?' I said. 'Can you keep an eye on Bob for a second?'

Handing Bob's lead to Rita, I took the bike and flipped it upside down to inspect it properly. The tyres were inflated and the chain looked like it was well oiled and moving pretty freely. The seat was a little low for me, so I adjusted it. Then I climbed on.

Bob was soaking up the sunshine on the pavement near Rita but kept half an eye on me throughout. He tilted his head to one side slightly, as if to say: *What's that thing and why are you sitting on top of it?*

'Bear with me, Bob,' I told him, as I gave the bike a quick spin.

The gears were a tad on the sticky side and, as Rita had warned me, the front brakes weren't working properly. I figured there was a problem with the wire inside the cable, which was easily fixed. The rear brakes were fine, however, which was all I needed to know.

'I'll give you a tenner for it, Rita,' I said, bringing the bike back.

'Deal,' said Rita, a little taken aback. 'You'll need this as well.'

She fished around under her trolley of magazines and produced a rather battered, old black cycle helmet.

The bike was one of the first, sensible investments I'd made in a while. I knew it would be useful back home in Tottenham, where I could use it for short journeys to the shops or the doctor's. I'd make the £10 back in saved bus fares in no time. For the longer journey to work, I'd carry on taking the bus or the tube. That journey was too treacherous to cycle, and full of notorious cycling accident spots.

Then something struck me. How was I going to get it home? Bus drivers don't let bikes on board, and there was no prospect of getting it on a tube.

There's only one thing for it, I told myself.

'OK, Bob, looks like you and I are riding this home,' I said.

He looked suspiciously at me again as I strapped on the cycle helmet, slung my rucksack on my shoulders and started wheeling the bike towards him.

'Come on, mate, climb on board,' I said, reaching down to him and letting him climb on my shoulders.

'Good luck,' Rita said.

'Thanks. I think we'll need it!' I said.

I walked the bike along the pavement for a while, towards Islington Memorial Green. We passed a couple of police officers who gave us a curious look, but said nothing. There was no law against riding a bike with a cat on your shoulders after all.

The looks on people's faces ranged from astonishment to hilarity. More than one person stopped in their tracks, pointing at us as if we were visitors from another planet.

When we reached the Green, we cut

across the corner past Waterstones bookshop and turned into Essex Road, the main road to north London.

'Here we go, Bob,' I said, bracing myself to enter the heavy traffic.

We started weaving our way through the buses, vans, cars and lorries. Bob and I soon got the hang of it. As I focused on staying upright, Bob decided, sensibly, to drape himself across my neck with his head down low and pointing forward. He clearly wanted to settle down and enjoy the ride.

It was mid-afternoon and a lot of children were heading home from school. All along Essex Road, groups of kids in uniforms stopped and waved at us. I tried waving back at one point but lost my balance a little bit, sending Bob sliding down my shoulder.

'Oops, sorry, mate. Won't do that again,' I said.

Progress was steady but slow at times. If we had to stop because of traffic, we were instantly shouted at by someone asking for a photo. At one point, two teenage schoolgirls jumped out into the road to snap themselves with us.

'This is so cute!' one of them said, leaning into us so heavily as she posed for her photo that she almost knocked us over.

I hadn't ridden a bicycle for a few years, and I wasn't exactly in prime physical condition, so I took a little breather every now and again, attracting a posse of onlookers each time I did so. Most smiled their approval but a couple shook their heads.

'Stupid idiot,' I heard one middle-aged guy in a suit say as he strode past us.

It didn't feel stupid at all. In fact, it felt rather fun. And I could tell Bob was having a good time too. His head was right next to mine and I could feel him purring contentedly in my ear.

I had been looking forward to the section of our journey where we headed towards Seven Sisters. At that point, the road dropped downhill for a mile or so. I'd be able to freewheel down it quite easily.

To my delight, there was a dedicated bike lane, which was completely empty. Bob and I were soon flying down the hill, the warm summer air blowing through our hair. We must have been going close to twenty miles per hour at one point.

'Woohoo! Isn't this great, Bob?' I said happily.

The traffic in the main lane to our right was gridlocked, and people were winding down their windows to let in some air. Some of the expressions on their faces as we whizzed past them were priceless.

A couple of children stuck their heads out of the sun-roofs of their cars and shouted at us. A few people just looked on in utter disbelief. That was understandable. You don't see a ginger cat whizzing down a hill on a bike very often.

It only took me about half an hour to get home. Pretty impressive, considering we'd had so many unplanned stops.

As we pulled up outside my block of flats, Bob just hopped off my shoulders like he'd been riding the bus. He had taken it all in his stride as just another routine day in London.

Back in the flat, I spent the rest of the afternoon and evening tinkering with the bike. I'd soon fixed the front brakes and given it a general tuning up.

'There you go,' I said to Bob, as I stood back to admire my handiwork. 'I think we've got ourselves a Bobmobile.'

I was pretty sure that the look he gave me signalled his approval.

Chapter 6
Body Language

People often ask me how Bob and I communicate with each other so well.

'It's simple,' I say. 'He has his own language, and I've learned to understand it.'

It might sound far-fetched but it's true.

Bob mainly uses body language. For instance, if he wants to go to the toilet when we are walking around the streets, he starts grumbling and growling. He then starts fidgeting on my shoulders. I don't need to look at him to know what he is up to. He's scouting around for a spot with some soft dirt where he can do his business.

If he is walking on his lead and gets tired, he lets out a light, low-pitched grumble or moan-cum-growl and refuses to walk another inch. He just looks at me as if to say, *Come on, mate, pick me up, I'm worn out.*

If he ever gets scared, he backs up on my shoulders. If he gets scared when he is standing on the ground, he reverses between my legs in case I need to pick him up. It is rare that anything frightens him though. Living and working in central London means the sound of an ambulance or a police car going by with their sirens blaring barely bothers him at all. The only thing that freaks him a little is the pressurised air brakes on big lorries and buses. Whenever he hears that loud, hissing sound, he recoils and looks scared. On bonfire nights, he also gets a little nervous about the loud bangs and explosions, but he generally enjoys watching the bright, sparkling lights in the sky from the window of my flat.

I can tell a lot about his mood from the way he moves his tail. If he is snoozing or asleep, his tail is still and quiet, of course. But at other times he wags it around. The most common wag is a gentle side-to-side movement, rather like a windscreen wiper on its slowest setting. This is his contentment wag. I've spent endless hours sitting around London with him and have seen him doing it when he is entertained or intrigued by something. The lady who tried to steal him at Angel wasn't the first person to misread this as a sign of anger. Bob does get angry but he signals that with a very different tail movement where he flicks it around, a bit like a fly swatter.

There are subtler messages too. If, for instance, he is worried about me, he comes up really close. If I am feeling ill, he often sidles up and listens to my chest. He does a lot of loving things like that. He has this habit of rubbing against me, purring. He also rubs his face on my hand, tilting his head so that I can scratch behind his ear. Animal behaviourists and zoologists are entitled to their opinions but, to me, this is Bob's way of telling me that he loves me.

Of course, his favourite subject is food. If he wants me to come to the kitchen to feed him, for instance, he goes around banging on the doors. He is so clever; he could easily unpick the child locks I've fitted on my food cupboards to keep him out, so I always have to go and check. By the time I get there, he has always moved to a spot by the radiator in the corner where he'll be wearing his most innocent look.

For a while, his biggest challenge was getting my attention while I played on the second-hand Xbox I'd picked up in a charity shop.

Bob was fascinated by certain video games, especially motor racing ones. On one occasion, I could have sworn I saw his body swaying as we took a particularly sharp hairpin bend together. He drew the line at action games with a lot of shooting, however. If I was playing one of these, he would head for another corner of the room. If the game – or I – ever got too loud, he'd lift up his head and look across. The message was simple: *Turn it down, please. I'm trying to snooze.*

Sometimes I could get really wrapped up in a game. Bob didn't appreciate this, especially when he was hungry, so he took more drastic measures.

I was playing a game with my friend Belle one night when Bob appeared. He'd had dinner a couple of hours earlier and had decided that he needed a snack. He went through his usual attention-seeking routine, making a selection of noises, draping himself across my feet and rubbing himself against my legs. But we were both so heavily involved in reaching the next level of our game that we didn't respond at all.

He sloped off, circling the area where the TV and Xbox were plugged in. After a moment, he moved in towards the control console and pressed his head against the big, touch-sensitive button in the middle.

'Bob, what are you up to?' I asked, still too engrossed in the game to twig what he was doing.

A moment later, the screen went black and the Xbox started powering down. Bob had applied enough pressure to the button to switch it off. We had been halfway through a really tricky level of the game, so we should have been furious with him. But we both sat there with the same expression of disbelief on our faces.

'Did he just do what I think he did?' Belle asked me.

Bob stood there looking triumphant. His expression said it all.

Let's see you try and ignore me now.

We don't always rely on signals and body language. There are times when we have a strange kind of telepathy. We've also learned to alert each other to danger.

A few days after I'd acquired the bike, I decided to take Bob to a local park. By now he was completely comfortable riding around on my shoulders, leaning in and out of the corners like a motor-bike pillion rider.

In the park, Bob was keen to explore. When I felt it was safe, I let him off his lead so that he could enjoy himself in the undergrowth while he did his business. I was sitting, reading a comic and soaking up a few rays of sunshine when, in the distance, I heard the barking of a dog.

Uh oh, I thought.

A very large, menacing German shepherd was running towards the park entrance. The dog was no more than a hundred and fifty yards away and was off its leash. I could tell it was looking for trouble.

'Bob!' I shouted at the undergrowth. 'Bob, come here!'

Bob understood what was happening immediately and bolted out of the bushes. He wasn't afraid of dogs but he picked his battles wisely. This wasn't a dog to pick a fight with.

Bob's bright ginger coat wasn't exactly hard to spot. I saw the dog accelerate towards us, barking even more fiercely. I had a terrible feeling that Bob had left it too late, so I grabbed the bike and got ready to ride it into the firing line if necessary. If the German shepherd intercepted him, Bob could be in serious trouble.

As so often in the past, however, I'd underestimated him.

He sprinted across the grass as I crouched down on one knee. In one seamless move, I flipped him on to my shoulders, jumped straight on to the bike and – with Bob standing on my shoulders – hit the pedals and began cycling out of the park.

The frustrated German shepherd

pursued us for a short time as we sped down the street. Bob was hissing at him. I couldn't see Bob's face, but it wouldn't have surprised me at all if he was taunting him.

What are you going to do about it now, tough guy? he was probably saying.

'That was a close one, Bob,' I said when at last we got clear. 'Thank goodness for the Bobmobile.'

Chapter 7
The Odd Couple

The intercom buzzer went just after 9am one weekday morning as Bob and I got ready for work.

'Who the heck is that?' I said, instinctively twitching at the curtains for a look even though I had no view of the entrance from up on the fifth floor.

'James, it's Titch. Can I come up with

Princess?' a familiar voice said over the speaker.

Titch was a tiny wiry bloke with short, thinning hair. Like me, he was a recovering addict who had started selling *The Big Issue*. He had been having a hard time lately, and had been 'de-badged' and given a six-month suspension for not showing up at work enough. I knew he was struggling to make ends meet.

I felt like I'd been given a second chance in life since I'd met Bob so I'd given Titch another opportunity as well. I also quite liked him. Deep down, I knew he had a good heart.

Another reason that Titch and I got on was that we both worked on the street with our pet as our companion. In Titch's case it was his sweet-natured black Labrador-Staffordshire bull terrier-cross,

Princess. Princess and Bob had never met though I braced myself for what might happen when Titch and Princess arrived at the front door.

When Bob saw Princess, he arched his back and hissed. Cats arch their backs to make themselves look bigger in a fight. They also make their fur stand on end for the same reason.

The moment Princess saw Bob in full, confrontational mode she froze to the spot.

'It's all right, Princess,' I said. 'Bob won't hurt you.'

I then led her into my bedroom and shut the door so that she felt safe.

'James, mate. Is there any way you can look after Princess for the day?' Titch said, cutting straight to the chase. 'I've got to sort something out.'

'Sure,' I said. 'Shouldn't be a problem. Should it, Bob?'

Bob gave me an enigmatic look.

'We are working at Angel today. Princess will be all right with us there, won't she?' I said.

'Yeah, no problem,' Titch said. 'So how about if I pick her up there this evening at about 6pm?'

It was all fixed.

'Be a good girl, Princess,' Titch said before heading off.

Bob didn't have a problem with dogs unless they were aggressive towards him so I wasn't worried about him. In our early days busking around Covent Garden, I'd seen him give one dog a bop on the nose with his paw.

Dogs were one thing. Cats were another. There were times when I wondered whether Bob knew he *was* a cat. He seemed to think they were inferior beings, unfit to breathe the same air as him. When money was tight, we'd walk to Angel rather than take the bus, and Bob would sniff and stare whenever we went past what was clearly a house that had cats inside.

If he ever saw another cat out and about he would let them know in no uncertain terms that this was his turf. Once, when he saw a tabby cat skulking around on Islington Green, Bob had strained so hard to get at the upstart invading his territory that it was like having an aggressive dog on the end of the lead. He had to stamp his authority on the situation. Obviously, he'd done the same with Princess.

I was a little worried that having

Princess that day would be a bit of an inconvenience. Dogs were much more hard work than cats. For a start, you couldn't put them on your shoulders as you walked down the street. It was a design flaw that, I soon discovered, slowed you down considerably.

Walking to the bus stop, Princess pulled on the lead, stopped to sniff random patches of grass and veered off to go to the toilet three times in the space of a couple of hundred yards.

'Come on, Princess, or we'll never get there,' I said, already regretting my decision.

On the bus, Bob took up his normal position on the seat next to the window and kept a watchful eye on Princess, who was tucked under my feet. The looks he gave Princess whenever she moved into his territory during the journey were hilarious. The area under the seat wasn't exactly spacious and Princess would occasionally wiggle to improve her position. Each time she did so, Bob gave her a look that said, *Sit still, you stupid dog.*

Outside the weather was atrocious, with rain hammering down. I took Bob to the little park at Islington Green to quickly do his business and decided to let Princess do the same. Big mistake. She took forever to find a suitable spot. I'd forgotten to bring any plastic bags with me so had to fish around in a rubbish bin to find something with which to scoop everything up. I really wasn't enjoying my day as a dog sitter.

With the rain getting heavier by the minute, I took shelter under the canopy of a café.

'Can I get a cup of tea, please?' I asked when a waitress appeared. 'And a saucer of milk for my cat and some water for the dog?'

The waitress smiled, like she served cats and dogs every day. 'Sure,' she said.

I then popped inside to use the toilet, leaving my two companions tied to the table with their leads.

When I got back, their positions had changed. I'd left them with Bob on a chair and Princess under the table. Now Bob was sitting on the table, lapping at his saucer of milk, while Princess was under the table looking far from happy with her bowl of water. Bob was top dog once again.

Despite the weather, Bob was still attracting attention from passers-by.

'Hello,' cooed a couple of ladies, stopping and stroking him.

It was as if poor Princess wasn't even there. I knew how she felt. I live in Bob's shadow sometimes.

But in the end, Princess proved very useful. She sat there, her eyes swivelling around like cameras, checking out everyone who approached us. If she liked the look of them, she stayed where she was. But if she didn't, she suddenly sat upright, and let out a little growl or even a bark. It was usually enough to get the message across.

If anyone knelt down to stroke and say hello to Bob, Princess would make sure that they were treating him with respect. She made my job a little easier.

It was often a challenge to keep an eye on Bob while trying to sell the magazine at the same time. The incident with the lady in the tweed suit had made me especially wary.

'Thank you, Princess,' I began saying, handing her a little treat from my rucksack.

Even Bob shot her a couple of approving looks. *Maybe she's not so bad after all,* he may have been thinking.

The weather remained miserable all afternoon, so when the clock started edging towards six, I started looking out for Titch. But 6pm came and went and there was no sign of him.

'Have you seen Titch?' I asked one of the *The Big Issue* co-ordinators.

'I haven't seen him for weeks,' she said, shaking her head.

By 6.30pm, I knew he wasn't coming.

'Come on, you two, let's head for home. Titch can collect you there, Princess,' I said, gathering all my stuff together.

I was a little worried. If Titch didn't come, how would Bob feel about having Princess for a sleepover? I imagined lots of barking, complaints from the neighbours and a sleepless night for me.

I bought Princess some dog food and doggie biscuits on the way home. As we all settled down to dinner in the kitchen, Bob put Princess in her place again. When she moved towards the bowl of water I'd laid out for her, Bob hissed and snarled loudly, forcing Princess to back off. He had to lap up his own bowl of milk first.

It didn't take them long to reach an agreement though. In fact, Bob allowed

Princess to clear out the remains of his dinner bowl.

I've seen it all now, I thought to myself. But I hadn't.

By 10pm I'd fallen asleep in front of the television. When I woke up, I saw something that made me wish I owned a video camera.

Bob and Princess were both splayed out on the carpet, snoozing quietly. Princess's head was barely a foot from Bob's nose. They looked like lifelong pals.

'Sleep well, guys,' I said with a grin.

I locked the front door, switched off the lights and headed off to bed, leaving them there.

The following morning, I was woken up by the sound of barking. It took me a moment to remember that I had a dog in the house.

'What's wrong, Princess?' I said, still half asleep.

Titch was at the door. From the look of his bleary face, he had slept rough.

'Really sorry to leave you in the lurch last night but something came up,' he said, apologetically.

I'd had nights like that myself, far too many of them.

'No problem,' I said.

Titch looked like he could do with something warm inside him.

'Do you want a cup of tea and some toast?' I asked.

Bob was lying next to the radiator, with Princess curled up a couple of feet away. The expression on Titch's face when he saw them was priceless.

'Look at those two,' I smiled. 'They get on like a house on fire now.'

'I can see it, but I can't quite believe it,' Titch said, munching on his toast. 'So would you mind looking after her again if I'm in the lurch?'

'Why not?' I said.

Chapter 8
The Garbage Inspector

We all have our obsessions in life. For Bob, it's packaging.

Bubble wrap offers endless entertainment. Who doesn't love popping the bubbles? Bob goes absolutely crazy with excitement whenever I let him play with a sheet of it. I always keep a watchful eye on him. Each time he pops a bit with his paw or mouth, he turns and gives me a look.

Did you hear that? he seems to say.

Wrapping paper is another fascination and he is also obsessed by the crispy, crunchy cellophane cereal comes in. He can spend half an hour rustling a ball of cellophane. Balls of scrunched-up aluminium kitchen foil have the same effect.

His absolute favourite, though, is cardboard boxes. If I ever walk past Bob with a cardboard box in my hand, he lunges at me as if to grab it. It doesn't matter whether it is a cereal box, a milk carton or a bigger box. He just bounds up, paddling his paws quickly.

Give me that, he seems to demand. *I want to play with it NOW.*

He also loves hiding in the bigger boxes. It's given me the heebie-jeebies on at least one occasion.

I don't let Bob wander out of our flat on his own and the windows are always closed to avoid him climbing out. I know cats can 'self-right' themselves in the air and we were 'only' five floors up, but I don't want to test his flying abilities! So when I couldn't find him in any of his usual spots one summer evening, I panicked slightly.

'Bob, Bob, where are you, mate?' I said.

I looked high and low, but there was no sign of him in my bedroom or in the kitchen or bathroom. Then it suddenly struck me. I'd put a box containing some hand-me-down clothes in the airing cupboard. Sure enough, I opened the cupboard to see a distinctive ginger shape deep in the middle of the box.

He did the same thing again not

long afterwards, with almost disastrous consequences.

Belle had come around to help me tidy the place up a bit.

'You have to chuck out some of this old tat,' she told me, looking around the flat at all the junk I'd collected over the years. I had lived there for a few years now and I like collecting things I found out and about.

So we organised a few cardboard boxes full of old books and maps and broken radios and toasters. We were going to throw some in the rubbish and take others to charity shops or the local recycling place.

Belle was taking one box down to the rubbish area outside the flats and was waiting for the lift to arrive when her box started jiggling around.

Aaargh! she screamed, more than a bit freaked out.

By the time I opened the door to see what the trouble was, she'd dropped the box and discovered Bob inside. He was pulling himself out from a collection of old books and magazines, where he'd curled up for a nap. It was a close shave – we almost threw him out with the rubbish!

Soon after that I made him a bed out of a cardboard box. I figured that if he slept in one, he might be less obsessed with them at other times. So I took one side off a box, then lined it with a little blanket.

'You're as snug as a bug in there, aren't you, Bob?' I told him when I saw him curled up inside.

He looked at me and purred. He loved it.

Bob was also deeply interested in the rubbish bin in the kitchen. Whenever I put something into the bin, he would get up on his hind legs and stick his nose in.

'What are you looking for, mate?' I would challenge him.

He would throw me a look as if to say, *That depends on what you're throwing in there. I haven't decided if I want to play with it or not.*

'I'll call you the garbage inspector, shall I?' I laughed.

I was just emerging from the bath one morning when I heard weird noises coming from the kitchen. I could make out a thin, metallic, scraping sound, as if something was being dragged around, together with a kind of low moaning.

'Bob, what are you up to now?' I said,

grabbing a towel to dry my hair as I went to investigate.

I couldn't help giggling at the sight that greeted me.

Bob was standing in the middle of the kitchen floor with an empty tin of cat food wedged on the top of his head. The tin was sitting at a jaunty angle on his head, right over his eyes.

It was obvious that he couldn't see much, because he was walking backwards across the kitchen floor, dragging the tin with him as he tried to reverse out of it. He was being very deliberate, occasionally wiggling the tin or raising it a little before giving it a tap against the floor in the hope the impact would knock it off his head. His plan wasn't working. It was comical to watch.

In the corner of the room I could see

the black bin liner containing the rubbish I was going to put in the wheelie
bins downstairs that morning. I normally emptied the bin and put the sack
out at night, to stop Bob playing with it.
But today I'd forgotten and left it on the
kitchen floor. Big mistake.

Bob had ripped and chewed at the
bottom of the bag to investigate what
was inside. No cardboard boxes but he
had found the old tin – and got his head
stuck inside. What a mess.

Wrow, he meowed. It was a sad and
pathetic little sound.

The tin had a serrated edge where it
had been opened, so I was careful in
removing it from his head. It was pretty
stinky, that was for sure.

The moment he was free, Bob scooted
off into the corner. There were bits of

food stuck to his ear and the back of his head, so he began licking and washing himself frantically, shooting me sheepish looks.

It wasn't the first time he'd done something like this. One day I heard another odd sound coming from the kitchen, a kind of tapping sound. *Pat . . . pat . . . pat* followed by a faster *pat, pat, pat, pat.*

Bob had been walking around with a miniature container of butter attached to one of his paws. He loved butter and had been dipping his paw inside the container so that he could lick it clean. He'd somehow wedged his paw inside and was now walking around with it on his foot. Every now and again, he'd raise his paw and tap it against a cupboard door in an effort to shift it. Eventually I'd had to help.

'Bob, you silly boy. What have you done to yourself?' I said, leaning down to help him again.

Yes, he seemed to say, *I know it was a dumb thing to do. Don't tell me you've never done anything stupid yourself.*

Chapter 9
Worms

Even though money was tight, I always tried to feed him good food in the recommended portions. In the morning, Bob had a flat teacup full of high-nutrition biscuits. And at the end of the day, about an hour before he went to bed, he'd have half a teacup of biscuits and half a pouch of meat as his evening meal.

He also had some little treats while we

were out working. It was always more than sufficient to keep him happy and healthy. In fact, he normally left a quarter or so of his morning biscuits because it was too much for him.

A few days after he'd got his head caught in the tin can, however, I noticed that he was wolfing down all his breakfast in double-quick time. He was even licking the bowl clean.

He was also more demanding. I had always decided when to give him a reward for his tricks, but now he began to ask for snacks himself. There was something different about the way he pleaded for these snacks as well. It wasn't the usual plaintive, 'Puss in Boots' look.

I'm desperate for food! he seemed to say.

It was the same when we got home. He began to hassle me as soon as we were in the door. Then he'd shovel every-thing down as fast as possible and give me a look straight out of *Oliver Twist.*

Please, Dad. Can I have some more?

The alarming thing, however, was that after a week or so of this behaviour, he wasn't gaining any weight.

That's odd, I thought to myself.

Bob was also going to the toilet more often. Over the years he'd overcome his dislike of going in the litter tray at home and did his business there in the morn-ings. He'd then go again when we were out in London. Suddenly, however, this habit changed. Now he was going three times or more each day.

Bob started demanding to be taken to the toilet more often at Angel. It was always a real palaver, packing up and heading over to the Green so that he could get on with things, but it had to be done.

'What is wrong with you, Bob?' I said, losing patience with him after a few days of this.

He just gave me an aloof look. *Mind your own business*, he seemed to say.

Then one day I saw him deep in concentration, scooting his undercarriage on the carpet in the living room.

I wasn't best pleased.

'Bob, that's disgusting,' I scolded him. 'What do you think you're doing?'

But I soon realised that it must mean that he had a problem.

As usual, I was short of money and didn't really have enough to splash out on the expense of a vet. So the next morning on the way into work, I decided to drop into the local library and look up

Bob's symptoms on the internet. I guessed he had some kind of stomach parasite. It was consistent with going to the toilet more often and scooting his bottom on the floor.

During my childhood in Australia, I'd seen a couple of cats develop worms. It wasn't pleasant, and was also contagious. A lot of children in Australia used to contract worms from their cats. It was quite gross actually. I really hoped this wasn't the case with Bob.

Researching illness on the internet is always the biggest mistake you can make. Within half an hour, I'd convinced myself that Bob had a really serious kind of worm: a hookworm or a tapeworm. Neither is fatal, but both are really nasty, causing severe weight loss and a deterioration in the coat if untreated.

I knew the only thing I could do to be sure was to check his poo the next time he went to the toilet. I didn't have to wait long. Within about an hour of us settling down at Angel, he started making his tell-tale noises and gestures and I took him off to the Green. I braced myself to sneak a quick look before he covered up his business in the soft earth.

He didn't take kindly to my intrusion.

'Sorry, Bob, but I've got to take a peek,' I said, inspecting his droppings with a twig.

It may sound bizarre, but I was delighted when I saw some tiny, white wiggly creatures in there. It *was* worms, but only tiny little ones.

At least it's not tapeworm or hookworm, I consoled myself for the rest of that day.

I felt a slightly confusing mix of

emotions. The responsible cat owner in me was really miffed. I was so careful about Bob's diet, avoiding raw meats and other risky things. I also regularly checked for fleas, which can act as hosts for worms. Bob was also a really clean and healthy cat, and I made sure the flat was in a decent condition for him to live. I felt like it reflected badly on me.

'I've let you down, haven't I?' I told Bob. 'But at least I now know what to do. We need to visit the vet, mate.'

The Blue Cross is an animal charity that looks after sick and injured pets, and I knew the Blue Cross drop-in van was going to be at Islington Green the following day. So I made sure that I got a sample of Bob's morning poo in a plastic pill container, and we got there early to beat the queue.

The staff there knew us well. Bob had been microchipped here, and I'd spent the best part of a year dropping in to slowly pay off the fees for that and other treatments. I'd also had him checked out frequently for fleas and other parasites, ironically.

'Can you describe the problem?' asked the vet who was on duty that morning.

'He's eating all the time, and going to the toilet a lot,' I explained. 'He's also itching his bottom on the floor. So I checked his poo and found worms.'

The vet checked the sample I had brought. 'Yes, he's got worms I'm afraid, James,' he said. 'What's he been eating lately? Anything out of the ordinary? Been rummaging in the bins or anything like that?'

It was as if a light had gone on in my head. I felt so stupid.

'Yes!' I gasped. 'He got his head stuck in an old food can a little while ago. He must have found a piece of old chicken or other meat in there!'

How could I have failed to see that?

The vet gave me a course of medication and a plastic syringe I could use to put the medicine down Bob's throat.

'How long will it take to clear things up?' I asked.

'Should be on the mend within a few days, James,' he said. 'Let me know if the symptoms persist.'

Years earlier, I'd had to give Bob some antibiotics by hand, putting tablets in his mouth and then rubbing his throat to help them on their way down into his stomach. The syringe was supposed to make that process simpler. But Bob still had to trust me to put it down his throat.

Back at the flat that evening, I could tell that Bob didn't like the look of the syringe. But he trusted me enough to let me place it inside his mouth and release the tablet.

'You know I wouldn't do anything to you that wasn't absolutely necessary, don't you, Bob?' I told him, rubbing his throat.

He seemed to understand.

Bob was back to his normal self within a couple of days. He was soon eating and going to the toilet normally again.

As I thought about what had happened, I gave myself a ticking off. The responsibility of looking after Bob had been such a positive force in my life. But I needed to live up to that responsibility a little better. Bob wasn't a part-time job that I could clock into whenever the mood took me.

'I must never let a bin bag lie around like that again,' I said to myself.

Most of all, though, I breathed a sigh of relief. It wasn't often that Bob was off colour or ill, but whenever he was I always jumped to the worst conclusions. Over the past days I'd imagined Bob dying and having to carry on life without him. It was too scary to think about.

I always said that we were partners, that we needed each other equally. Deep down I believed that wasn't really true. I felt like I needed him more.

Chapter 10
Cat on a Hoxton Roof

Bob and I are a distinctive pair. There aren't many six-foot-tall blokes walking around the streets of London with a ginger cat sitting on their shoulders, after all.

For a few months during the summer and autumn of 2009, we made an even more eye-catching sight. Unfortunately, I was in too much pain to enjoy the attention.

The problems had begun the previous year, when I travelled to Australia to see my mother. My mum and I had always had a difficult relationship. Apart from a brief visit to London, the last time I'd seen her was when she'd seen me off at the airport aged 18 to 'make it' as a musician in London. In the lost decade that followed, we'd barely talked. Time had healed the wounds a little, so, when she offered to pay for me to visit her in Tasmania, I went.

With Bob's help, I'd just managed to make a massive breakthrough with my drug addiction. It had left me feeling weak, so I needed the break. Bob had stayed with my friend Belle, at her flat near Hoxton in north London, not too far from Angel.

There was always a risk of DVT

– deep vein thrombosis – when you were tall like me and sat without moving on a flight for hours. I had known about the risks, but despite doing my best to walk around the plane as often as possible, I'd come home with a nagging pain in my upper thigh.

At first it was manageable, and I dealt with it by taking ordinary painkillers. Slowly but surely, however, it grew worse. I began feeling as if my blood had stopped flowing and my muscles were seizing up. I felt as if I had the leg of a zombie.

The pain soon became so bad that I couldn't sit or lie down in a normal position. So whenever I was watching television or eating a meal at home in the flat, I had to sit with my leg on a cushion or another chair. At bedtime, I had to sleep the wrong way round with my foot raised up over the end of the bed head.

I went to see the doctor a couple of times, but they had only prescribed stronger painkillers. I'm sure they felt that my condition, whatever it was, was left over from my drug-abusing past. I didn't push it, but it reinforced that old feeling I'd had as a homeless person that I was invisible.

The real problem for me was that I still needed to earn a living. However uncomfortable I was, I still had to haul myself out of bed and head to Angel on a daily basis.

It wasn't easy. The moment I put my foot on the floor, pain shot up through my leg. I could only walk three or four steps at a time. So the walk to the bus stop became a marathon, often taking me twice or three times as long as it would normally.

Bob didn't know what to make of this at first. He kept giving me quizzical looks, as if to say, *What are you doing, mate?* But he soon worked out there was something wrong and started changing his behaviour.

In the morning, for instance, rather than greeting me with his usual pleading looks, he started looking at me with a slightly pitying expression.

Feeling any better today? he seemed to ask.

He began to walk alongside me rather than ride on my shoulders. He obviously preferred travelling on the upper deck, as I put it, but I think he could see I was in pain.

When he felt that I had been hobbling

along for too long, he would actually try to make me stop and sit down. He would cut across my path, steering me towards a bench or wall where I could take a break. I thought it was better to finish my journey rather than stopping every few steps so, for a while, it developed into a bit of a battle of wills.

Whenever he heard me complain about the pain, Bob would stop and give me a look.

Take a breather or sit down then, he seemed to say.

'No, Bob,' I would reply. 'I need to keep moving.'

If I hadn't been in so much agony, I'd probably have found it quite amusing to watch. We probably resembled a bickering old married couple.

To make life easier, I began staying

with Belle. Her flat was on the first floor rather than the fifth floor, which saved me a lot of aggravation. Getting to work from Belle's place was also less painful with a bus stop only yards away.

But the pain continued to grow worse.

'I need a crutch,' I decided one morning.

With Bob in tow, I'd headed into the pretty little park near Belle's flat and found a branch from a fallen tree that fitted perfectly under my arm. It allowed me to keep the weight off my painful leg when I walked.

I got a lot of very strange looks, understandably. With my long hair and shaggy beard, I must have looked like some kind of modern-day Merlin. The ginger cat sitting on my shoulders must have conjured up images of wizards walking around with their 'familiars'. The truth was that I didn't really care. Anything that eased the pain was a Godsend.

The Bobmobile was in the hallway back in Tottenham, gathering dust. There was no way I could cycle anywhere with the pain I was in.

Bob understood that there was something seriously wrong with me. Some mornings, as he watched me struggling to get my trousers on, he would give me a withering look.

Why are you doing this to yourself? he seemed to say. *Why don't you stay in bed?*

'I have no option, Bob,' I said through gritted teeth. 'We're skint, as usual.'

Standing at my pitch outside Angel tube station for five or six hours a day was becoming impossible.

Fortunately, one of the tube-station

florists saw the state I was in one day and came over to me, holding a couple of buckets that he used for his flowers.

'There you go, sit on that. And get Bob to sit on the other one,' he had said, giving me an encouraging pat on the back.

'Thanks,' I said gratefully. 'I really appreciate it.'

When I started sitting on the bucket, I was terrified that people simply wouldn't see me sitting there and I wouldn't sell any magazines. I should have known better. Bob took care of it.

During this period, he became a real little showman. He would rub up against me and give me a look, as if to say *Come on, mate, get the snacks out. Let's do some tricks and earn a few quid!*

I was certain he'd worked out that the

sooner we earned a decent amount of money, the sooner we could get home and rest my leg. It was eerie how he understood so much.

I wished I could see life so clearly sometimes.

Living at Belle's with Bob had its pros and cons. While I spent as much time as I could off my feet, Belle looked after me, cooking me nice meals and doing my laundry. Bob got on well with her too. During the time he'd spent with her while I was in Australia, they had clearly formed a strong bond. She was the only other person whom he would ever consider allowing to pick him up, for instance.

The previous year, when Bob had run

away from Angel one evening after being attacked by a dog, he'd headed for Belle's flat. It had taken me hours to work out that he'd taken refuge there. It had been the longest night of my life.

The closeness of their relationship certainly made life easier for me. But it also gave Bob licence to be mischievous.

One morning I got up and headed into the kitchen in my T-shirt and boxer shorts to make myself a cup of coffee, expecting to find Bob settled there. There was no sign of him. There was no sign of Belle either.

It had been raining heavily that morning but it was now bright and sunny and the temperature was rising. I noticed that Belle had already opened the window in the kitchen to let some fresh air into the flat.

'Bob, where are you, mate?' I said, searching the flat.

There was no sign of him in the sitting room or the hallway, so I headed to the back bedroom where Belle slept. When I saw the window there was ajar, I got an instant sinking feeling.

Belle's flat was on the first floor and the back bedroom window overlooked the roof of the extension on the ground floor flat below us. That roof overlooked a yard and the car park for the building. From there it was a short walk to the main road, one of the busiest in that part of London.

'Oh, no, Bob,' I gasped, squeezing my head out of the window. 'You haven't gone out there, have you?'

Sure enough, five flats along from Belle's, there was Bob, sunning himself on the roof.

'Bob!' I yelled in alarm. I was concerned that he might slide off the slippery roof, or go down into the yard and out through the car park on to the main road.

He slowly turned his head in my direction.

What's wrong? he seemed to say.

Chapter 11
Asking Questions

I panicked and took the security screws off the window, so that I could open it fully and climb out on to the roof. I still hadn't managed to put on any clothes.

The slate tiles were slippery from the rain earlier in the morning, so keeping a grip wasn't easy. I was in agony with my leg. Somehow, however, I managed to cross the rooftops to where Bob was sitting.

I was on a wasted mission.

Bob instantly picked himself up and scuttled back across the rooftops. When I tried to grab at him, he just growled at me and made a sudden spurt towards Belle's open window, disappearing back indoors.

It took me a few minutes to scramble back across the slippery slates. To my complete embarrassment, a couple of faces appeared in the windows. The looks on their faces spoke volumes. They were a mix of shock, mild pity and hilarity.

Moments after I got back into the safety of the flat, I heard the front door closing. Belle was standing in the hallway with a small bag of groceries.

She burst out laughing.

'Where have you been?' she giggled.

'On the roof trying to rescue Bob,' I said.

'Oh, he goes out there all the time,' she said. 'He even goes down into the yard sometimes. He always comes back up.'

'I really wish you'd told me that sooner,' I complained, shuffling off to finally put on some clothes.

Soon after that, it was Belle who was suffering from Bob's playful ways.

As I'd discovered the hard way, Bob loved exploring the back of Belle's block of flats. He took full advantage of the fact that he was on the first rather than the fifth floor.

I knew that it was part of Bob's DNA to hunt. Cats are seriously effective predators. One day we were sitting in the front room when he arrived with a small mouse dangling from his mouth. He'd placed it carefully at my feet, as if he was offering me a gift.

'Bob, you will make yourself sick again if you eat that,' I scolded.

He soon became bolder.

One morning, I was lying on my bed reading when I heard the most almighty scream.

Aaargh!

I jumped up and ran into the living room where Belle was doing some ironing. There, sitting on top of a pile of freshly pressed shirts and bed sheets, was a little brown frog.

'James, James, pick it up, get rid of it. Please,' she shrieked.

Bob was in the doorway with a

mischievous expression on his face. It was as if he knew exactly what had happened.

I got hold of the little frog and cupped it in my hands. I then walked round the area at the back of the building to release it, with Bob following me every step of the way.

About an hour or so later, I heard another scream, accompanied by the sound of something hitting a wall.

'What is it now?' I said, heading into the hall.

Belle was standing at one end of the corridor with her hands on her head and a horrified expression on her face. She pointed down the corridor at a pair of slippers that she'd clearly thrown down the hallway.

'It's inside my slipper now,' she said.

'What's inside your slipper?' I said, puzzled.

'The frog.'

I had to suppress a laugh. But, again, I retrieved the frog and took it out to the garden. Again Bob marched behind me, trying to look like it was a pure coincidence that this frog had now appeared inside the flat twice.

'Stay there, mate,' I said. I had to make sure I disposed of the frog properly this time.

Bob looked at me disapprovingly, then turned and slinked off back into the house as if to say, *you're really no fun at all!*

As comfortable as we were at Belle's, after a while I began to realise that it wasn't ideal, in particular for my relationship with Bob.

The pain in my leg had made me short-tempered and generally less fun to be around than usual. Sensing that I wasn't in the best of moods when I woke up, Bob wouldn't always come into the bedroom for an early morning play. Often Belle would rustle up a breakfast for him instead. He would also head off out of the window to hunt and would sometimes be gone for long stretches. I imagined he was having a great time out there.

I also had a very strong suspicion that he was eating elsewhere too. When Belle or I put down a bowl for him, he did little more than play with his food.

At first my heart sank a little. *He's eating in the bins again*, I said to myself.

One day, when we were heading out to work, I saw an elderly gentleman downstairs, collecting his mail. Bob saw him and fixed him with a knowing stare.

'Hello, young fellow,' the man said. 'Nice to see you again.'

Suddenly I remembered that children's book *Six Dinner Sid* by Inga Moore, about a cat that charms its way into the affections of everyone on his street, earning himself a dinner in every house each night. Bob had pulled the same stunt. He had become Six Dinner Bob.

It was a sign that Bob was getting used to life without me at the centre of his world. Lying there at night, trying to think about anything and everything but the throbbing pain in my leg, I began to ask myself something I'd not asked in all the time Bob and I been together. Would he be better off without me?

Who needed to be out on the streets in all kinds of weather, being poked and prodded by passers-by? Especially when there were friendlier, less complicated souls around to give you a square meal every day.

I'd always felt that I could give Bob as good a life as anyone else. Now, for the first time since we'd got together, I wasn't so sure.

Chapter 12
Bob's Choice

Another time, I was limping through the car park in a local supermarket when I saw a wheelchair, sitting there unoccupied. The thought of being able to travel around without having to put any weight on my foot was really tempting. For a split second, I thought about stealing it. I was ashamed of myself the moment the idea entered my head.

I also found myself thinking more and more about Bob. Or more specifically, losing Bob. The worse my leg became, the more I became convinced that he was ready to leave. I imagined him in the company of the old man next door, being pampered and fussed over. I pictured him lying on the sunny roof at Belle's while I hobbled off to sell *The Big Issue* on my own.

Because of the pain, I had less patience for Bob than usual and wouldn't play with him. Sometimes he would try to drape himself around my leg, which I found unbearable. By now my leg was a violent, red colour and the pain was relentless.

'Go away and play somewhere else, Bob,' I'd say, brushing him to one side.

He'd reluctantly head out of the

bedroom door, throwing me a disappointed look as he went.

*It's hardly a surprise that he's starting to
look elsewhere for affection*, I thought. *I'm
not much of a friend to him at the moment.*

At last, one morning I woke up and
decided that enough was enough. I
didn't care what the doctors thought
about me and my past: I wanted some
answers. I wanted this problem to go
away. I got dressed, grabbed my crutch
and headed for the local surgery.

'That's an interesting crutch you have
there, Mr Bowen,' the doctor said when
I turned up in the consulting room.

'Necessity is the mother of invention,'
I said.

He began casting an eye over my thigh
and leg.

'This doesn't look too good,' he said.

'You need to keep pressure off that leg for a week or so and you need a blood test to check for clotting in the blood cells.' He looked at my crutch. 'And I think we can do better than a tree branch.'

By the end of the morning I was the proud owner of a pair of proper metallic crutches, complete with rubber grips, arm holders and shock absorbers. I didn't waste any time and went to have the blood test done the following day.

A couple of days later, I rang the clinic.

'Any news on my blood test?' I asked.

The female doctor confirmed my worst suspicions.

'You have a deep vein thrombosis, or DVT. It means you have a blood clot in your leg. So I need you to go to University College Hospital for tests,' she told me.

In a way it was a relief. I'd always suspected the long flight to and from Australia had caused the problem. But it was worrying too. I knew that DVT could cause heart attacks and strokes in particular.

When I got to the hospital I was told that, sure enough, I had a large blood clot in my leg.

'The hot weather probably set it off and then you made it worse by walking around on it,' said the doctor. 'I'll give you some medicine that should sort it out.'

I was relieved. But I didn't pay any attention to the leaflet that came with the medicine that explained about certain side effects.

A few nights after I started taking the tablets, I woke up to find my leg was covered in blood. The sheets of my bed were soaked red as well.

Bob had been fast asleep in the corner, but woke up. He could tell there was something wrong and shot up to stand at my side.

'I have to get to a hospital,' I told him, 'and fast.'

I threw on a pair of jeans and a jumper and ran out of the flat, heading towards Tottenham High Road where I figured I had a chance of catching a bus.

When I got to the hospital, they admitted me immediately. I was kept in for two days while they sorted out my medication.

'We'll try another drug,' said a doctor. 'It shouldn't have the same effect.'

But it didn't work. Even after a couple of weeks, my leg was no better. I couldn't walk more than two paces, even with the crutches. I was now beginning to despair. Once again, I began to imagine losing my leg altogether.

I went back to the hospital.

'Help me,' I begged.

This time they decided to keep me in for a week to check me out more thoroughly.

'Come back tomorrow,' they said. 'We'll have a bed for you then.'

I wasn't best pleased about it. But I knew that I simply couldn't carry on in this condition. I went home that night and explained the situation to Belle.

'I'll look after Bob,' Belle assured me.

This was a huge comfort. I knew Bob was happy in Belle's flat. The following morning I got up and packed a small bag of stuff to take to hospital.

I'm not the greatest hospital patient. I lay there worrying about everything – my leg, my long-term health, my pitch at Angel and, as always, the lack of money. I also lay there and fretted about Bob.

I could see that I'd not been the most brilliant company in recent weeks. Maybe it was time for us to go our separate ways. Should I ask Belle if she wanted to keep him? Or the nice bloke next door? I would be devastated to lose him. He was my best friend, my rock. I needed him to keep me on the straight and narrow, to keep me sane. But at the same time, I had to make the right choice for Bob. I really didn't know what to do.

Then it struck me. It wasn't my decision.

They say cats choose you, not the other way round. For whatever reason,

Bob had seen something in me that made him want to stick around. Now I had to wait to see if he'd choose me again. If he wanted to remain with me, then it would be his decision. And his alone.

I'd find out his answer soon enough, I felt sure.

Chapter 13
The Final Step

The doctors in the hospital increased the dose of my medicine and they also decided to keep me in a little longer.

'Just for a couple more days,' the doctor told me. 'We want to make sure it works this time.'

The new dosage finally sorted out my DVT. When I looked at my leg the swelling was beginning to go down and the

colour returning to normal. The nurses
and doctors could see this as well.

'It's not good for you lying there all
day, Mr Bowen,' one of the nurses kept
saying to me. 'Try walking up and down
the corridor at least a couple of times a
day.'

It was a joy to be able to walk around
without wincing so much. It still hurt,
but it wasn't anywhere near as bad as
before.

'I think it's time to go home,' smiled
one of the doctors.

I texted Belle with the good news.

'Great!' she texted back. 'I'll meet you
at the hospital later.'

By the time I'd filled in the paperwork,
got dressed and gathered together my
belongings, it was nearly evening.

'Meet me outside by the art sculpture,'

Belle texted. 'Can't come into hospital. Will explain when I see you.'

I limped my way to the exit on Euston Road. I'd heard people at the hospital talking about the art sculpture outside: a giant, six-ton polished pebble. I leaned on it for a moment or two as I tried to catch my breath, after walking what seemed like miles along the corridors without the aid of crutches.

I soon saw Belle emerging from the bus stop across the road. She was carrying a large, holdall style bag which, I assumed, had some clean clothes and my jacket in it.

As she got closer, I saw a flash of ginger fur poking out of the unzipped top of the bag. Then, as she reached the bottom of the hospital steps, I saw a little head poking out.

'Bob,' I said, excited.

The moment he heard my voice, Bob began scrambling out of the bag. We were still a few feet apart when he launched himself off the bag towards me. It was the most athletic leap I'd ever seen him make, and that was saying a lot.

'Whoaah there, fella,' I said, lurching forward to catch him and holding him close to my chest.

He pinned himself to me like a limpet clinging on to a rock that was being pounded by waves. He then nuzzled his head in my neck and started rubbing me with his cheeks.

'Hope you don't mind, but that's why I couldn't come in. I had to bring him,' Belle said, beaming. 'He saw me packing a few things for you and started going crazy. I think he knew I was coming to get you.'

Whatever doubts I'd had about our future together were swept away in that instant. On the way home, Bob was all over me – literally. He sat on my lap, crawled on my shoulders and sat up with his paws on my chest, purring away contentedly.

It was as if he never wanted to let me go again. I felt exactly the same way.

'I thought Bob wanted to leave me,' I told Belle.

'Far from it,' she laughed. 'The whole time you were in the flat, he was desperate to help you. Didn't you realise?'

Belle told me that whenever I had been asleep in my room, Bob would check up on me.

'He'd give you a little tap on the

forehead and wait for you to react. I think he just wanted to make sure you were still with us,' she smiled.

At other times, she told me, he would wrap himself around my leg.

'It was like he wanted to take away the pain,' she said. 'He was definitely trying to do something about it.'

I hadn't realised any of this. Instead, whenever Bob had tried to help or comfort me, I'd driven him away. I'd been selfish. Bob loved – and needed – me as much as I loved and needed him. I wouldn't forget that.

A few weeks after getting back on my feet, I took the most important step I'd made in years. Perhaps in my entire life.

I'd been attending a drug clinic for several years now. I'd arrived there a mess, addicted and on a fast track to an early grave. Thanks to a brilliant collection of counsellors and nurses, I'd been hauling myself back from the brink ever since. I had started taking a prescription drug that I needed before I could come off drugs altogether. It had been a pretty seamless process, much easier than I'd anticipated.

'A few more days of taking it,' explained my drug counsellor, 'and I think you'll be ready to call yourself clean.'

I should have been delighted. It was time for that soft aeroplane landing that one of my counsellors had talked about. But I was curiously on edge, and remained that way for the next two days. It was almost as if I was waiting for something awful to happen.

Bob sensed that I needed a little more TLC. He wasn't obvious about it. He didn't need to perform any of his late night diagnoses or tap me on the head to check I was still breathing. He just sat a few inches closer on the sofa and gave me an extra rub of his head on my neck every now and again.

Five or six days after I had been given my final prescription, I pulled the foil container out of its packet and saw that there was just one tablet left.

I squeezed the oval-shaped pill out, placed it under my tongue until it had all dissolved, and then downed a glass of water. I scrunched the foil up into a ball and threw it on the floor for Bob to chase.

'There you go, mate,' I said. 'That's the last one of those you'll get to play with.'

That night, I felt sure that my body was going to be racked by withdrawal pangs. I expected nightmares, visions, restless twisting and turning. But there was nothing. The moment my head hit the pillow, I was out like a light.

When I woke up the next morning, I gathered my senses and thought to myself: *That's it. I'm clean.*

I looked out of the window at the London skyline. It wasn't a glorious blue sky, unfortunately. But it certainly was a clear one. And it seemed somehow brighter.

I knew that the days, weeks, months and years stretching ahead of me weren't going to be easy. There would be times when I knew that niggling temptation would return, and I'd think about taking something to deaden the pain, to kill the senses.

Loneliness and hopelessness had driven me to drugs in the first place. But I was determined that wasn't going to happen again. Life wasn't perfect, far from it. But it was a million times better than it had been when I'd formed my addiction. I could see a way forward. I knew that I could soldier on.

From that day onwards, each time I felt myself weakening I told myself: *Hold on. I'm not sleeping rough, I'm not alone, it's not hopeless. I don't need drugs any more.*

A month or so after I'd taken that last tablet, my drug counsellor signed me off.

'I don't need to see you again,' he said as he ushered me out of the door. 'Stay in touch, but good luck. And well done.'

And I am happy to say I have not had to see him since.

Chapter 14
Big Night Out

As we walked south across the Thames at Waterloo Bridge, the lights of the Houses of Parliament and the London Eye blazed bright in the late November night sky and the pavement was busy with people. It was approaching 10.30pm, the end of their day. For me and Bob, on the other hand, it was the beginning of what promised to be a very, very long night.

The Big Issue was staging an event called 'The Big Night Out' to coincide with the eighteenth birthday of the magazine. They were organising an eighteen-mile walk through the streets of London in the middle of the night to mark the occasion.

The idea was that ordinary people could walk through the deserted city between 10.30 pm and 7am with a group of *The Big Issue* vendors, so that they could learn a little about the reality of living rough and sleeping on the streets.

I'd made the decision to take part for a couple of reasons. Firstly, it was a chance to earn a few extra pounds. Every vendor that took part in the walk was eligible for 25 to 30 free copies of *The Big Issue*. That meant that I could earn about £60 if I sold them all.

Secondly, it was an opportunity to talk to people about the magazine and the lives of the people who sold it. *The Big Issue* was, without question, the salvation for many people who lived on the streets. It had certainly helped give me direction and purpose – not to mention enough money to keep the wolf from the door. It was important to share that with people.

We were meeting at the IMAX cinema on the south side of Waterloo Bridge. It was a fitting location. Not so long ago, the area had been home to the shanty town that Londoners knew as Cardboard City. During the 1980s and early 1990s, it had become a home for more than 200 'rough sleepers'. Many people created homes for themselves just from wooden pallets and cardboard boxes. Some even had living rooms and bedrooms with mattresses. I'd stayed there briefly during its final days, at the end of 1997 and early 1998, when everyone was evicted to make way for the IMAX cinema.

My memories of the place were sketchy, but when I walked into the IMAX I saw the organisers of the walk had created a little picture exhibition on the history of Cardboard City. With Bob on my shoulders, I scanned the grainy black and white images for faces that I recognised. As it turned out, I was looking in the wrong place.

'Hello, James,' a female voice said behind me. I recognised it straight away.

'Hello, Billie,' I said.

Back around the year 2000, when my life was at its lowest ebb, Billie and I had become friendly, helping each other out and keeping each other company. We had huddled up against the cold together at the cold-weather shelters that charities like Centrepoint and St Mungo's used to put up during the winter months.

'How's it going, Billie?' I said.

'Good,' she told me. 'I've turned my life around.'

Billie told me how she had been sleeping rough in central London ten years earlier when she was disturbed from her sleep by a seller of *The Big Issue*.

'At first I was annoyed at being woken up by him,' she said. 'I hadn't even known what the magazine was. But then I looked at it and grasped the idea.'

Billie had managed to rebuild her life. Now she was a 'poster child' for The Big Issue Foundation.

We reminisced about the bad old days over a cup of tea. It was hard to remember that time because it was all a blur. But we were still here. Goodness knows how many of the people who had been on the streets with us hadn't been so lucky.

Billie was very committed to this walk.

'It will give people an idea what we had to go through,' she said. 'They won't be able to slip off home into a warm bed. They'll have to stay out there with us.'

Billie had a dog, a lively Border collie called Solo. Solo and Bob weighed each other up for a few minutes but then decided there was nothing to worry about.

Just before 10.30pm John Bird, the founder of *The Big Issue*, arrived. He fired everyone up with an inspiring speech about the difference the magazine had made during its eighteen years. By now a hundred or more people had gathered, along with a couple of dozen vendors, co-ordinators and staff. We all filed out into the night, ready for John Bird to do the countdown.

'Three, two, one,' he shouted and then we were off.

'Here we go, Bob,' I said, making sure he was positioned comfortably on my shoulders.

On the one hand, I was really worried about whether my leg would stand up to eighteen miles of wear and tear, but, on the other, I was just delighted to be off my crutches and walking normally again. So, as we set off on the first leg around the South Bank and across the Millennium Bridge, I told myself to simply enjoy it.

As usual, Bob was soon attracting a lot of attention. There was a real party atmosphere, and a lot of the charity fundraisers began taking snaps of him as we walked. He wasn't in the friendliest of moods, which was understandable. It was way past his bedtime and he could feel the cold coming off the Thames. But I had a generous supply of snacks as well as some water and a bowl for him. I'd also been assured there would be a bowl of milk for him at the stop-off points.

We will give it our best shot, I said to myself.

Chapter 15
Calling It Quits

Bob and I settled into a group in the middle of the procession as it worked its way along the riverside. They were a mix of students and charity workers, as well as a couple of middle-aged women. One of the ladies started asking me questions.

'Where do you come from?' she asked. 'How did you end up on the streets?'

'I came to London from Australia when I was eighteen,' I explained. 'I was born in the UK, but my parents separated and my mum took me with her when she moved down under. We moved around a lot and I became a bit of a troublemaker. When I came to London, I hoped to make it as a musician but it didn't really work out. That's when my troubles started and I ended up on the streets, and that's where *The Big Issue* came in.'

After about an hour and a half, we made it to the first stopping-off point – the Hispaniola floating restaurant on the Embankment on the north side of the Thames.

I helped myself to some of the soup on offer, while Bob lapped up some milk that someone had kindly sorted out for him. I was feeling pretty positive about the walk now and was already totting up the miles that I'd done – and how many more were to come.

But then, as we were heading off the ship, we had a bit of a setback. Perhaps because he knew that my leg still wasn't a hundred per cent, Bob decided to walk off the boat instead of riding on my shoulders. As he padded his way down the ramp, he walked straight into another vendor who was coming up the walkway with a dog, a Staffie.

The Staffie instantly went for Bob.

'Whoa!' I said, and jumped in front of it with my arms and legs out to stop him lunging at Bob.

Staffies do get a bad reputation for being violent, but I don't think this one was. He was just being curious, not evil. Unfortunately, however, it freaked Bob out a bit. As we started our walk again, he wrapped himself tightly around me. I think this was partly because he was nervous but also to protect himself against the cold. There was a bone-chilling mist rising off the Thames.

'I think we might go home,' I told a couple of the organisers. I was worried about Bob now, especially as the weather looked to be getting worse.

'Stay a bit longer,' they persuaded me. So we did.

As we headed away from the river, the temperatures lifted a little bit. We wound our way through the West End and headed north. I got talking to a pretty young blonde girl and her French boyfriend.

'How did you and your cat get together?' they wanted to know.

Talking about Bob suited me fine and we had a really nice chat together for the next part of the walk. But as the night wore on, I began to feel a throbbing pain in my thigh, where the DVT had been. It was inevitable. But it was still annoying.

For the next hour or so I ignored it. But whenever we stopped for a cup of tea I could feel an acute shooting pain. Bob and I had been falling further and further behind, eventually reaching the back of the line. And after taking a couple of breaks to let Bob do his business, suddenly I realised that we had cut loose from the rest.

The next official stop was a few miles away. I really didn't think I could make it that far. So when we passed a bus stop with a night bus that headed in our direction, I made a decision.

'What do you think, Bob, shall we call it quits?'

Bob didn't say anything, but I could tell that he was ready for his bed. When a bus loomed into view and opened its doors, he bounded on board and on to a seat, bristling with pleasure at being in the warm.

The bus was surprisingly busy given how late it was. Bob and I were surrounded by a cluster of clubbers, happy from their night out in the West End or wherever it was they'd been. There were also a couple of lonely-looking guys, sitting there as if they were on the road to nowhere. I'd been there and done that, of course. I not only had the T-shirt, I had a wardrobe full of them.

But that was the past. Tonight it felt very different. Tonight I felt rather pleased with myself. Walking a dozen or so miles might not have seemed much of an achievement to some people but, for me, it was the equivalent of running the London Marathon.

I'd also been reunited with some familiar faces. It had been a joy to see Billie again and to see how well she was doing. All in all, I felt like I'd done something positive, that I'd given something back. I'd spent so many years taking from people, because I thought I had nothing to give. Tonight had shown me that wasn't true. Everyone has something to contribute, no matter how small. Maybe tonight, I'd opened a few people's eyes to the reality of life on the streets. That wasn't to be dismissed. It was worth something.

And so, I began to quietly tell myself, was I.

Chapter 16
A Tale of Two Cities

I drew back my bedroom curtains and looked out across the north London rooftops. Thick banks of iron-grey clouds were stacked up overhead and I could hear the wind gusting and whistling outside. If ever there was a day to stay at home and wrap up warm, today was that day. Unfortunately, that wasn't a luxury I could afford.

Things were tight at the moment. Both the gas and electric meters needed topping up, so the flat was icy cold. Bob had started snuggling up close to my bed at night, hoping to soak up some of the heat from my duvet. The bottom line was that I had to keep selling *The Big Issue*, and I couldn't afford to take the day off.

The only question was whether Bob was going to come with me. As always, it would be his decision. It was a decision he generally got right.

Cats – like a lot of other animals – are very good at 'reading' the weather and other natural events. They are very skilled at predicting earthquakes and tsunamis, for instance. Bob certainly sensed when rain was in the air. He hated getting wet and often refused to come out when the weather seemed fine, only for the heavens to open an hour or two later when I'd taken to the streets on my own.

So when I showed him his lead and scarf and he came towards me as normal, I guessed that his weather forecasting instincts were telling him it was safe to venture out.

'You sure about this, Bob?' I said. 'I'm happy to go on my own today.'

I picked out one of his thickest and warmest scarves. Then I wrapped it snugly around his neck and we headed out into the greyness.

The moment I set foot on the street outside, the wind cut through me like a scalpel. I felt Bob's tummy curling itself even tighter than usual around my neck.

Fortunately our regular bus service

appeared within a few minutes, and Bob and I were soon on board. Feeling warmth on the back of my leg from a heater lifted my spirits briefly. But things soon took a turn for the worse.

We'd barely been on the road for ten minutes when I noticed the first flakes of snow swirling around outside. Within moments, the air was thick with chunky, white flakes that were already sticking to the pavement and the roofs of parked cars.

'This doesn't look good,' I said to Bob, who was absorbed by the transformation that was taking place on the streets outside.

A mile or so from Angel, the traffic had ground to an almost total standstill. I faced a real dilemma. It was going to be tough to earn a few quid today, and conditions were going to be really challenging. But at the same time, I was short of money. I wasn't sure I had enough to get back home, let alone put a few quid in the electricity meter over the next day or so.

'Come on, Bob, if we're going to earn anything today we'd better walk the last mile,' I said, reluctantly.

We hopped out on to the pavement. For Bob, this was a fascinating new world to explore. I had put him on my shoulders as usual, but I'd barely walked a few yards before he was repositioning himself ready to clamber down to earth.

As I put him down, I realised that it was the first time Bob had been out and about in snow. I watched him dabbing a paw into the powdery whiteness, then standing back to admire the print he'd left behind. For a moment I imagined what it must be like to see the world through his eyes. It must have seemed so bizarre, to see everything suddenly turned white.

'Come on, mate, we can't hang around all day,' I said after a minute or two.

Bob was still having a great time lifting his feet in and out of the ever-deepening snow. Eventually, however, it got so deep that his belly was lined with white crystals.

'Let's get you back up here,' I said, grabbing him and sticking back on my shoulders.

The problem now was that the snow was falling so steadily and heavily that it was settling on both of us. Every few yards I had to brush an inch of fresh snow off my shoulders, then do the same thing to Bob.

I had a broken old umbrella but it was next to useless in the strong winds. I gave up on it within minutes.

'This is no good, Bob. I think we need to find you a coat,' I said.

I dived into a small convenience store, stamping my feet clean of snow in the doorway.

At first the owner, an Indian lady, looked shocked to see the pair of us standing there. This was hardly surprising. We must have made a bizarre sight. But her mood soon thawed.

'You are brave walking about in this weather,' she smiled.

'I don't know about brave,' I said. 'Mad might be closer to the truth.'

I wasn't quite sure what I was looking for. At first I wondered about buying a new umbrella, but they were too expensive. I only had a small amount of change. But then I had an idea and headed for the area where the kitchen supplies were stocked. I saw a roll of small, heavy-duty bin liners.

'That might do the trick, Bob,' I said. 'How much for a single bag?' I asked the lady.

'I can't sell them as singles. I have to sell you the whole roll. It's £2,' she said.

I didn't want to fork out that much. I really was broke. But then I noticed she had little black carrier bags on the counter top for customers to carry their shopping.

'Is there any chance I could take one of those?' I said.

'OK,' she said. 'They are 5p.'

'I'll take one,' I said. 'Do you have any scissors?'

'Scissors?'

'Yes, I want to make a hole in it.'

This time she looked at me as if I truly was off my rocker. But she dipped down behind the counter and produced a small pair of sewing scissors.

'Perfect,' I said.

I grabbed the closed end of the bag and cut a small semicircle about the size of Bob's head. I then opened the bag up and slipped Bob's head through it. The improvised poncho fitted like a glove and covered his body and legs perfectly.

'Oh, I see,' the lady said, laughing. 'Very clever. That should do the trick.'

It took us about fifteen minutes to get to Angel. One or two people shot us funny looks as we walked along, but most were more concerned with getting themselves from A to B safely in the drifting snow.

I knew there was no way we were going to be able to survive outside the tube at our normal selling pitch. The pavement was thick with slushy snow. So Bob and I positioned ourselves in the nearest underpass where the bulk of commuters were taking refuge.

I didn't want to keep Bob out in the cold for too long, so I put some extra effort into selling the magazines I had. Fortunately, a lot of people seemed to take pity on us and dipped into their pockets. My pile of magazines was soon dwindling.

By late afternoon, I'd made enough cash to keep us going for a day or two.

'Now, all we've got to do is get home,' I said to Bob as we once more bent ourselves into the icy winds and headed back to the bus stop.

Working on the streets of London really was a tale of two cities, as I was reminded again a few days later.

I was standing just outside Angel tube station around lunchtime, with Bob on my shoulders, when I noticed a bit of a commotion going on inside at the ticket gate where passengers emerged from the trains below. A group of people were having an animated conversation with the attendants. When it was over, they started heading in our direction.

I recognised the large, slightly scruffy, blond-haired figure at the centre of the group immediately. It was the Mayor of

London, Boris Johnson. He was with a young boy, his son I assumed, and a small group of smartly dressed assistants. They were marching straight towards my exit.

'How about a *Big Issue*, Boris?' I said, waving a magazine in the air.

'I'm in a bit of a rush,' he said, looking flustered. 'Hold on.'

To his credit, he started digging around in his pockets and produced a pile of coins, which he dropped into my hands.

'There you go,' he said. 'More valuable than British pounds.'

I didn't understand what he meant, but was grateful nevertheless.

'Thanks very much indeed for supporting Bob and me,' I said, handing him a magazine.

As he took it, he smiled and tilted his head slightly at Bob.

'That's a nice cat you've got there,' he said.

'Oh yes, he's a star,' I said. 'He's even got his own travelcard.'

'Amazing,' he said, before heading off.

'Good luck, Boris,' I said as he disappeared from view.

Chapter 17
Trouble on the Street

I hadn't wanted to be rude and check what Boris Johnson had given me a moment or two earlier, but, judging by the weight and number of the coins, it felt way more than the cover price of the magazine.

'That was generous of him, wasn't it, Bob?' I said, fishing around for the coins, which I'd hurriedly stuffed in my jacket pocket.

As I looked at the small pile of cash, however, my heart sank.

'Oh no, Bob,' I said. 'He gave me Swiss francs! That's what he meant when he said *more valuable than British pounds*.'

Except, of course, they weren't more valuable.

While foreign bank notes can be exchanged at most banks and *bureaux de change*, coins cannot. They were worthless. To me, at least.

It wasn't the first time something like this had happened to me.

A few years earlier, I'd been busking in Covent Garden when a very grand-looking character with a mane of grey hair reached into his trouser pocket and pulled out a scrunched-up note. It was red and looked like a big denomination, possibly a £50 note. That was the only note I knew that had red in it.

'There you go, my man,' he said, thrusting it into my hand.

'Thanks very much indeed,' I said.

I waited a few minutes until he had gone before studying the scrunched-up note more closely.

It wasn't a £50 note. As I'd thought, it was red, but it had a picture of a bearded bloke I'd never seen before on it. It also had the number 100 written on it and was covered in some kind of Eastern European language. The only word that looked familiar was *Srbije*. I had no idea what it was or what it might be worth. So I packed up my stuff and headed for a shop that I knew changed foreign money and was open late for tourists.

'Can you tell me what this is worth,

please?' I said to the girl who was behind the window.

She was puzzled. 'I don't recognise it,' she said. 'Let me check with someone else.'

She went into a back office where I could see an older bloke sitting. After a short conversation she came back.

'It's one hundred Serbian dinar,' she said.

That sounded hopeful.

'It's worth just over 70p,' she said. 'So we can't exchange it.'

I felt disappointed. I'd secretly hoped that it might be enough money to get me and Bob through the weekend. Fat chance.

I was fed up with living off my wits on the streets. And I was fed up with being humiliated by those who had absolutely no idea of the life I was having to lead. There were times when I was close to breaking point. A few days after that incident with the Mayor, I felt like I had reached it.

Bob and I finished work early and took the tube to Victoria Station. As we weaved our way through the tunnels, Bob walked ahead of me on his lead. He knew we were going to meet my father.

Meeting my dad was something I'd begun to do more regularly in recent months. Spending a lot of my childhood in Australia meant I didn't see him much, but we'd become closer when I'd started cleaning up my act, and had got into the habit of meeting for a few drinks and a meal at a pub at Victoria Station. The staff there were pretty friendly and would let me slip Bob in provided I kept him hidden from the other punters. I'd learned to keep him under a table where he was happy snoozing. It was always my dad's treat. Well, I was never going to have the money to treat him, was I?

As usual, he was waiting there for me.

'So what's your news?'

'Not a lot,' I said. 'I'm getting cheesed off with selling *The Big Issue*. It's too dangerous. And London is full of people who don't care about you.'

'You need to get yourself a proper job, Jamie,' he said. (He was the only person who called me that.)

'That's easier said than done, Dad,' I said.

My dad was a hard worker who had

always been his own boss. I don't think he understood why I hadn't been able to do the same thing. To his credit, he'd tried to help but it hadn't panned out. He had remarried since splitting with my mum, and had two children, my half-siblings Caroline and Anthony, to look after. It got complicated.

'What about training in computing or something like that? There are loads of courses around,' he said.

This was true, but I didn't have the qualifications to get on most courses.

My dad said he'd ask around to see if there was anything going. 'But things are pretty rough everywhere at the moment,' he said, holding up a copy of the evening paper. 'Every time I look at the paper it's all doom and gloom. People losing their jobs everywhere.'

I knew he was frustrated by the way I lived my life. Deep down I knew he felt I wasn't trying. I understood why he felt that way, but the truth was that I was trying. Just in my own way.

To lighten things up a little we talked a bit about his family and my half-brother and -sister.

'What are you doing for Christmas?' he asked at one point.

'I'm just going to spend it with Bob,' I said. 'We enjoy being together.'

My dad didn't really get my relationship with Bob. Tonight, as usual, he stroked him occasionally and kept an eye on him when I popped to the toilet. He even got the waitress to bring him a saucer of milk and gave him a couple of snacks. But he wasn't a natural cat lover. And on the one or two occasions when I had talked about how much Bob helped me in sorting myself out, he just looked baffled. I suppose I couldn't blame him for that.

We spent an hour and a half together, but then he had to catch a train back to south London. He gave me a few quid to tide me over and we agreed to see each other again in a few weeks' time.

'Look after yourself, Jamie,' he said.

The station was still busy. I had a few magazines left in my satchel so decided to try and shift them before heading home. I found an empty pitch outside the railway station and was soon doing pretty well.

Bob had a full stomach and was on good form. People were stopping and making a fuss. I was just weighing up whether to stay or head home when trouble reared its head again.

I knew the men were going to be a problem the moment I set eyes on them heading across the road towards the main entrance to Victoria Station. I recognised one of them from my days selling *The Big Issue* in Covent Garden. His mate wasn't familiar, but I could tell he was a rough character. He was a big brute and was built like a sack of potatoes.

I was worried that they were heading in our direction. Sure enough, they were soon outside the tube station entrance. The bigger of the two men made a beeline for me. He was every bit as aggressive as he looked.

'Oi, you, get lost,' he said, sticking his big red face close to mine. His breath stank.

Bob, as always, had spotted the danger and was hissing at him already. I wasn't going to be intimidated and stuck my ground.

'I've got a right to sell here and I've just got these few magazines to sell,' I said. 'You know you don't have any magazines and all you're looking to do is intimidate people – what you are doing is wrong. I've seen you beg before. You are nothing but a leech. I know you're forcing your mate to beg for you too.'

'You've got two minutes to pack your stuff up and leave,' he said. He then pushed his way into the crowds.

People were flooding in and out of the station, so I lost him and his mate for a few minutes. I was hoping that they were going to disappear. No such luck.

In hardly any time, the big guy reappeared, looking even angrier than before.

'Didn't you hear what I told you?' he snarled.

The next thing I knew he had hit me. He just walked up to me and punched me on the nose. It happened so fast, I didn't even see him pull back his arm. He just jabbed a giant fist into my face. I didn't have a hope of deflecting the blow.

Blood came gushing out of my nose. Bob meowed in concern.

I decided this wasn't a fight I could win. There was no sign of the police, so I was on my own against a pretty nasty pair of individuals. Working on the streets was risky, I knew that. But at times like this, it was downright dangerous.

'Come on, Bob, let's get out of here,' I said.

I felt a mix of anger and despair. I

couldn't take much more of this life. But I couldn't see how on earth I was going to break free. Suddenly, all that talk with my father of jobs and training seemed ridiculous. Who was going to give me a job and pay me a decent salary? On that day, feeling as low as I did, the answer was as plain as the bloodied nose on my face: no one.

Chapter 18
Two Cool Cats

One lunchtime in September 2010, I arrived at Angel tube to be greeted by a woman called Davika. She was a ticket attendant and had been one of our most loyal friends since Bob and I had started working in Islington. She often brought Bob a little treat or something to drink, especially during hot weather. Today, however, she simply wanted to deliver a message.

'Hi, James, there was someone here looking for you and Bob,' she said. 'He was a reporter from one of the local papers. He asked me to call him back if you were willing to talk to him.'

It wasn't the first time someone had paid us attention. There were a couple of films on the internet about me and Bob that had been viewed by a few thousand people and a couple of London bloggers had written nice things about us, but no one from the newspapers had shown any interest. To be honest, I took it with a pinch of salt.

A couple of days later, however, I found this guy outside the Angel tube station waiting for us.

'Hi, James, my name is Peter,' he said.

'I was wondering if I could do an interview with you for the *Islington Tribune*?'

He took a picture of Bob perched on my shoulders with the Angel tube station sign behind us. I felt a bit self-conscious. I hadn't exactly dressed up for the occasion and had a thick, early winter's beard, but he seemed happy enough with the results.

We then had a bit of a chat about my past and how Bob and I had met.

'Great,' he said, when he'd finished asking questions. 'The article will appear in the next edition of the *Tribune.*'

I didn't really take it too seriously. I'd believe it when I saw it. It was easier thinking that way.

A few days later, Rita and Lee, the co-ordinators at *The Big Issue* stall on Islington Green, called me over.

'Hey, James, you and Bob are in the paper today,' Rita said, producing a copy of the *Tribune*.

Sure enough there was a half-page article on us written by Peter Gruner. The headline read:

TWO COOL CATS . . .
THE BIG ISSUE SELLER
AND A STRAY CALLED BOB

The story began:

> Not since the legendary Dick Whittington has a man and his cat become such unlikely celebrities on the streets of Islington. *The Big Issue* seller James Bowen and his docile ginger cat Bob, who go everywhere together, have been attracting comments since

they first appeared outside Angel tube station. The story of how they met — widely reported in blogs on the internet — is one of such extraordinary pathos that it seems only a matter of time before we get a Hollywood film.

I had to laugh out loud. Dick Whittington? Hollywood film? And I wasn't terribly pleased with the way I looked in the photo, sporting that thick beard. But it was a lovely piece, I had to admit.

I popped into the newsagent's and grabbed a few copies to take home. Bob did a kind of double take when he saw the picture. For a split second he had this slightly baffled expression on his face. It was as if he was saying, *No, it can't be. Can it? Really?*

In the days that followed the article, more and more people started saying hello to us, not only at Angel, but on the bus and on the street.

One morning I was taking Bob to do his business on Islington Green when a group of schoolchildren appeared in front of us. They could only have been about nine or ten years old and were in very smart, blue uniforms.

'Look, it's Bob,' a boy said, pointing excitedly.

'Who's Bob?' said one of his friends.

'That cat there on that man's shoulders. He's famous. My mum says he looks like Garfield,' the boy said.

I was touched but I thought the comparison with Garfield, the world's best-known cartoon cat, was unfair. Garfield was obsessed with eating and very lazy. Bob had always been in good shape, ate pretty sensibly and had the friendliest, most laid-back attitude of any cat I'd ever met. And no one could ever call him work-shy.

Our most significant encounter, however, came from someone I'd spoken to once before.

I was approached one evening by an American lady.

'My name's Mary,' she said, 'and I am a literary agent. I live nearby and have noticed you outside the tube station many times. Have you considered writing a book about your life with Bob?'

I said I would think about it, but I hadn't taken her seriously. How could I? I was a recovering drug addict who was struggling to survive selling *The Big Issue*. I didn't write a diary. I didn't even write texts on my mobile phone. Yes, I loved to read, and consumed all the books I could lay my hands on. But *writing* a book was about as realistic as building myself a space rocket.

Fortunately, Mary had persisted, and we'd spoken again.

'Why don't you meet with a writer who is experienced at helping people tell their stories?' she suggested, guessing my concerns. 'I know the right guy. He's busy at the moment, but I'll fix for him to come and see you soon.'

After the *Islington Tribune* piece Mary contacted me again.

'Are you happy to meet this writer I have in mind?' she asked. 'If he thinks there is a book in Bob and you, he will spend time with you, getting you to tell your story. He'll help to shape it up and write it. Then I'll try and sell it to a publisher.'

Again, it sounded too far-fetched for words.

I didn't hear anything for a while. Then, towards the end of November, I got a call from this writer guy. His name was Garry.

I agreed to meet him and he took me for a coffee in the Design Centre across the road from my pitch. We had Bob with us, so we had to sit outdoors in the biting cold. Bob was a better judge of character than me, so I made a point of going to the toilet and leaving them alone a couple of times. They got on famously, which I took to be a good omen.

I could tell Garry was trying to work out whether my story was suitable for a book. As we spoke, he said something that struck a chord.

'I can see that Bob and you were both broken souls,' he said. 'You came together when you were both at rock bottom. You helped mend each other's lives. That's the story you have to tell.'

I had never thought of it in those terms. Instinctively, I knew that Bob had been a hugely positive force in my life. I'd even seen that there was a video on YouTube that someone had filmed of me where I said that Bob had saved my life. I guessed that, to some extent, it was true. But I just couldn't imagine *that* being a story that would interest anyone.

Even when I had seen Garry again for another, longer chat, it all seemed a bit of a pipe dream. There were so many ifs and maybes. If Garry and Mary were willing to work with me, maybe a publisher would be interested in releasing a book. I really couldn't see all three of those things happening. As the festive season and the end of the year loomed into view, I told myself there was more chance of Father Christmas being real.

During the run up to Christmas, Bob and I were given a host of presents. Bob's favourite was an advent calendar filled with treats. He quickly learned to make a fuss first thing in the morning when it was time for me to produce the latest snack on the countdown to Christmas.

We also got a fantastic Santa Paws outfit. Belle had made me one for our very first Christmas together but it had somehow got lost. This one had a snug red jacket and a very striking red hat for Bob to wear during the festive season. Passers-by at Angel were besotted by it.

On Christmas Day itself Bob spent more time playing with the wrapping paper than his actual presents. I left him to it and spent the afternoon watching television and playing video games. Belle popped round for a few hours too. It felt like a real family Christmas to me.

A couple of weeks into the New Year I got a phone call from Mary.

'A major London publisher, Hodder & Stoughton, want to meet you, James,' she said. 'And Bob, of course.'

A few days later, we went along to their offices in a rather grand tower block near Tottenham Court Road. At first, the security people wouldn't let Bob into the building. They looked baffled when we said he was going to be the subject of a book. I could see their point. What on earth would Hodder be doing publishing a book about a scruffy-looking bloke and his ginger tom cat?

In the end, Bob was treated like visiting royalty. He was given a goodie bag with some little snacks and catnip toys and allowed to explore the offices. Wherever he went he was greeted like some kind of celebrity. People were snapping away on their phones and cooing over him.

'I knew you had star quality, Bob,' I told him with a laugh, 'but I didn't realise it would be quite this good.'

I, on the other hand, had to sit in a

long meeting, talking about everything from marketing and publicity to production and sales. The long and the short of it was that they had seen some of the material Garry and I had worked on and they wanted to publish a book based on it. Between them, they'd even come up with a title: *A Street Cat Named Bob*.

'Come and visit my literary agency in Chelsea,' Mary suggested.

Again, it was a very grand and slightly intimidating place. There were a few odd looks when people realised that a *The Big Issue* seller and his cat had walked in. While Bob explored the offices, Mary ran me through the contract that I'd been offered by the publishers.

'It's a good deal,' she said, 'especially as you're an unknown author.'

I placed my trust in her and signed all

the paperwork. It felt weird scrawling my name, but also very, very exciting. This couldn't really be happening. Not to me.

Chapter 19
Start at the Beginning

I began meeting Garry once or twice a week in Islington. This suited me really well because it meant that I could top up my money by spending a few hours working afterwards. But it also meant that I had Bob with me. This meant that finding somewhere to sit and talk was a challenge, especially when the weather was bad. The local cafés wouldn't let a cat on the premises and there wasn't a library nearby. So we had to find alternatives.

The first people to invite us in from the cold were Waterstones, the bookshop on Islington Green. They knew me in there. I'd often popped in with Bob to look through the Science Fiction section. The manager there, Alan, was on duty one day when I was with Garry.

'Do you mind us working upstairs in a quiet corner?' I asked him.

He not only said yes, he got a member of staff to organise two chairs for us in the History section. He even brought a couple of coffees in.

Garry and I were determined that the book wouldn't just be about my life with Bob. We wanted it to offer people some insights into life on the streets. I wanted to show how easy it was for people like me to fall through the cracks, to become forgotten and overlooked by society. Of course, in order to do that, I had to tell my 'back story' as well.

I wasn't looking forward to that part. Talking about myself wasn't something that came easily to me, especially when it came to the darker stuff. But once we began talking, to my surprise, it was less painful than I'd feared. It forced me to confront some painful truths and helped me to understand myself a little better.

I knew I wasn't the easiest person to deal with. I had a defiant, self-destructive streak that had consistently got me into trouble. I'd always tried really hard to fit in and be popular as a kid, but it had never worked. I'd ended up trying too hard – and become a misfit and an outcast as a result.

On a happier note, I had some wonderful people helping me at the time and I remembered how I had wanted to give something back so had begun donating boxes of comic books to a hospital I'd gone to. I'd managed to get myself some work experience in a comic book shop nearby and persuaded the boss to let me take boxes of unsold magazines for the other kids there. I'd spent many hours playing air hockey and watching video games in the activity room they had in the children's ward so I knew they'd all appreciate something decent to read.

In the main, however, I didn't have great memories of being a child.

I knew I couldn't blame the doctors, my mother or anyone else for the way my life had gone since then. I made mistakes

of my own free will. I hadn't needed anyone's help to screw up my life – I'd done a
perfectly good job of that on my own.

If nothing else, the book was an opportunity for me to make that crystal clear.

When I showed him the cheque I'd been
given for the book, my dad was lost for
words. The expression on his face was a
mixture of disbelief, happiness, pride –
and mild apprehension.

'That's a lot of money, Jamie,' he said
after a couple of moments. 'You'd better
be careful with that.'

The reality hadn't really sunk in until
now. Not just for my dad, but for me
either. There had been meetings with
publishers, contracts signed, even articles

in the newspapers. But it hadn't been until I received this cheque for the advance that it finally struck home.

When it had first flopped through the letterbox a couple of days earlier, I had opened the envelope and then simply sat there looking at it. The only cheques I'd seen in the past decade had been for small amounts, £50 here and £100 there, never anything with more than a couple of noughts on it.

Compared to some people, especially in London, it wasn't actually that large a sum of money. For a lot of the commuters walking past me each day on their way to the City of London, I guess it wasn't even a month's salary. But for me, it was an eyewatering amount of cash.

The arrival of the cheque, though, had brought two immediate problems. I was terrified of frittering it away. But I also didn't have a bank account into which I could pay it. Which was why I'd travelled to my father's house in south London.

'I was hoping you could look after it for me,' I asked him over the phone. 'I can then ask you for money as and when I need it.'

Dad agreed. Rather than meeting as usual at Victoria, he'd invited me over to his neck of the woods. We went for a couple of drinks in his local and chatted for a couple of hours.

'So is this going to be a proper book?' he asked me.

'What do you mean?'

'Well, is it a picture book or a children's book? What is it going to be about exactly?' he said.

'It's the story of how I met Bob,' I explained, 'and how we helped each other.'

He looked a little nonplussed. 'So will me and your mother be in it?' he asked.

'You might get a mention,' I said. 'But don't worry. The only person that comes out badly in all this is me.'

That made him change tack a little.

'Is this going to be a long-term thing?' he continued. 'You writing books?'

'No,' I said, honestly. 'I'm not going to become the next J.K. Rowling, Dad. There are thousands of books published every year. Only a tiny minority of them become bestsellers. I really don't think a tale about a busker and his stray ginger cat is going to be one of them. It's a nice windfall, but no more.'

'All the more reason to be careful with the money then,' he said.

He was right, of course. But when he went off into a lecture about various investments and savings schemes, I tuned out completely.

Chapter 20
Fun and Trouble

Being with Bob has been such an education. He has taught me as much, if not more, than any human I've come across. I've learned important lessons about everything from responsibility and friendship to selflessness. He has even given me an insight into a subject I thought I'd never really understand – parenthood.

Caring for Bob has made me realise that parenthood is all about anxiety. Whether it is fretting over his health, watching out for him when we are out on the streets, or simply making sure he is warm and well fed, life with Bob often feels like one worry after another.

It actually chimes with something that my father had said to me after we'd lost contact for a time. It had been at the height of my addiction, and both he and my mother had been beside themselves with concern about me.

'You have no idea how much a parent worries about his or her child,' he had shouted at me. 'It's so selfish, not getting in touch with us.'

It hadn't meant much to me then. But since being with Bob, I have come to understand what he meant. I wish I could turn back the clock and save them all that grief.

That is the bad news. The good news is that 'parenthood' brings a lot of laughter with it too. For far too long I'd found it hard to find much joy in life. Bob has taught me how to be happy again. Even the slightest, silliest moments we share together can bring an instant smile to my face.

One Saturday lunchtime, for instance, I answered a knock on the door and found the guy from the flat across the hallway standing there.

'Hi,' he said. 'I just thought I'd let you know that your cat is out here.'

'Must be someone else's. Mine's in here,' I said, turning around to scout around the living room. 'Bob. Where are you?'

There was no sign of him.

'No, I'm pretty sure this is him out here. Ginger, isn't he?' the guy said.

I stepped out into the hallway to discover Bob sitting perfectly still on top of a cupboard on the landing, with his head pressed against the window, looking down on the street below.

'He's been there a while. I noticed him earlier,' the guy said, heading for the lift.

Bob looked at me as if I was the world's biggest party pooper. The expression on his face seemed to say: *Come on up here and take a look at this view with me, it's really interesting.*

Belle was visiting and was in the kitchen rustling up a sandwich.

'Did you let Bob out?' I asked. 'I can't work out how he got out into the hallway and hid himself up on top of the cupboard.'

'I popped downstairs about an hour ago to put some rubbish out,' Belle said, remembering. 'He must have slid out without me noticing, and then hidden away somewhere when I came back up. I'd love to know what's going on in his mind sometimes.'

I couldn't help laughing out loud. I'd wondered the same thing on many occasions.

There was nothing Bob loved more than watching the world go by. He would regularly sit on the kitchen windowsill, monitoring the goings on below, like some kind of security guard.

His head would follow people as they walked towards and then past our block of flats. If someone turned into the entrance to the building, he'd stretch his neck until he lost sight of them. I found it incredibly entertaining. It was almost as if he had a list of people who were allowed to travel this way at certain times and in certain directions.

He'd see someone passing and look as if to say, *Yes, OK, I know who you are*, or, *Come on, you're running late for the bus to work*. At other times he'd get quite agitated, as if he was thinking: *Oi, hang on! I don't recognise you!* or *You don't have clearance, where do you think you're going? Get back here.*

Bob loved playing hide-and-seek too. I'd found him hiding in all sorts of surprising nooks and crannies. He particularly loved anywhere warm.

One evening, I went to have a bath before I went to bed. As I nudged the bathroom door open, I couldn't help thinking it felt a little odd. Rather than swinging open easily it needed an extra nudge. It felt heavy somehow.

I didn't think much more of it and started running a bath. I was looking in the mirror by the sink when I noticed something moving on the back of the door amongst the towels I kept in a rack. It was Bob.

'How on earth have you got up there?' I said, howling with laughter.

I worked out that he must have climbed on to a shelving unit near the door and then jumped on to the towels. It looked pretty uncomfortable as well as precarious, but he seemed really happy.

Another frequent trick was to hide inside the clotheshorse I often used to dry my washing in the bathtub, especially during winter.

Several times I'd been in the bathroom and suddenly noticed the clothes moving. Bob would push the clothes apart like curtains, his face wearing a sort of *peek-a-boo* expression. He thought it was great entertainment.

Bob's antics often got him into trouble.

He loved watching television and computer screens. He could while away endless hours watching wildlife programmes or horse racing. So when we walked past the gleaming new Apple store in Covent Garden one afternoon, I thought I'd give him a treat. The place was bursting with shiny new laptops and desktops, none of which I could afford. But the Apple philosophy was that anyone could stroll in and play with their technology. So we did.

We had spent a few minutes playing with the computers, surfing the internet and watching YouTube videos when Bob spotted a screen that had a kind of aquarium-style display, with exotic and really colourful fish swimming around. I could see why he was attracted to it. It was absolutely stunning.

I took him over to the giant screen and let him gape at it for a few moments. It was funny to watch. He would follow a particular fish as it moved across the screen and then disappeared. He would then do a sort of double take and dart behind the giant screen, expecting to find the fish there. Then he'd dart back again and start following another fish.

It carried on like this for a few

minutes until I turned around to see his paw wrapped around a white cable. He was pulling on it and was threatening to drag one of the giant consoles with him.

'Oh, Bob, what are you doing?' I said.

A couple of Apple 'geniuses' were standing there laughing.

'He's a star, isn't he?' one of them said.

'If he breaks anything, I'm afraid you'd have to cover the costs,' said a more senior member of the team.

Given the prices of the products on display in the store, I wasted no time in untangling him and getting out of there.

Chapter 21
The Joy of Bob

When Bob and I first got together, he
didn't like going down the escalators and
lifts on the underground and especially
hated the crowds there during the rush
hour. Over the years, however, he has
conquered his fears ... and now it has
become somewhere he likes to misbehave!
He even has his own travelcard, given to
him by the staff at Angel tube station.

Now he travels just like any other Londoner, going about his or her business. He trots along the tunnels, always walking close to the wall for security. When we get to the platform, he stands behind the yellow line, unflustered when the train pulls into the station, despite the noise it makes. He then waits patiently for the doors to slide open before padding quietly on board and checking for an empty seat.

Even the most ice-hearted commuters melt when they see him sitting there. They snap away with their camera phones, then head off to work smiling. Living in London can be tough. The idea that we are somehow lightening people's days cheers me up.

Travelling on the tube has its perils, however.

One evening we'd headed home from

central London on the tube to Seven
Sisters, the nearest tube station to my
flat. As we were coming up the escalator,
I noticed Bob's tail was sticky and coated
in a black, tar-like material. The stuff
was on his body too.

I was at a loss to know what it was
exactly. It looked like engine oil or some
sort of heavy grease. But I did know that
it was potentially harmful.

Bob seemed to have worked this out
as well. He'd spotted the mess and had
already decided that giving it a lick
wasn't a good idea.

My phone was low on credit but I had
just about enough to make a call. I rang
a friend, Rosemary, a vet who had helped
us out once before when Bob had been
ill. She loved Bob and was always willing to help.

'Bob is covered in some kind of engine oil,' I told her. 'What should I do?'

'You need to wash it off right away,' she advised. 'Motor and engine oil can be highly toxic to cats. It can cause really bad inflammation and burning of organs, especially the lungs. It can also cause breathing problems, seizure and even death in really bad cases.'

'You're scaring me,' I said, feeling uneasy.

'You really need to wash it off him,' she repeated. 'If it doesn't come off, you should take him to the Blue Cross or another vet first thing in the morning. Does Bob let you bathe him?'

Cats seem to fall into two categories when it comes to bath time: there are those who hate it and those who love it. Luckily, Bob falls well and truly into the second camp. In fact, he is a bit obsessed with his bath.

He loves nothing more than climbing into the tub when I run a bath. He has learned that I always run a warm bath rather than a steaming hot one and hops into the tub so that he can paddle around in it for a few minutes.

It is funny – and, of course, very cute – to watch him walking around afterwards as he lifts and shakes one paw at a time.

He also gets very possessive about the bath plug and steals and hides it. I end up using a makeshift plug, only to find the real plug lying on the living room floor where Bob has been playing with it.

Sometimes I have to put a jug with a weight on it over the plug to stop him from stealing and hiding it.

So given all that, it was no problem getting him into the bath so that I could get this mystery grease off his tail.

I didn't have to hold him down. I used both hands to rub his tail and his side using some cat-friendly shower gel. I then hosed him down with the shower head. The expression on his face was hilarious: a mix of a grimace and a grin. Finally I dried him with a towel. He loved it and was purring throughout.

I popped into the Blue Cross at Islington later that week and got them to give him a quick check up, just in case. They told me there was nothing to worry about.

'Easier said than done,' I said to the nurse. 'There's always something to fret about with this one.'

I realised afterwards that I sounded a little like a parent.

In the years since we'd found each other, Bob had become domesticated – but only to a certain degree. When it came down to it, he remained a stray cat at heart.

My gut feeling is that he must have spent a large part of his young life living off his wits on the streets. He is a Londoner, born and bred, and is never happier than when he is exploring it. I often smile to myself and say, 'You can take the cat out of the street, but you can't take the street out of the cat.'

Bob has a few favourite haunts. At Angel, he loves visiting Islington Memorial Green, the little park where he is free to rummage around in the bushes, sniffing out whatever catches his interest while he does his business. There are a few overgrown corners where he can discreetly disappear for a few moments of privacy. Not that privacy bothers him too much.

He is also very fond of the grounds of St Giles in the Fields churchyard just off Tottenham Court Road. Often, when we walk from our bus stop on Tottenham Court Road towards Neal Street and Covent Garden, he starts moving around on my shoulder.

I want to stop at St Giles, he seems to tell me. *I want to check it out.*

The graveyard at St Giles is an oasis in the middle of one of the busiest parts of the city, with benches to sit and watch the world go by. For some reason, Bob's favourite toilet spot there is in full view of the street, by a set of railings on a wall. He is unfazed by the flood of Londoners passing by and often quietly goes about his business there.

When we were working on Neal Street, Bob's preferred toilet spot was outside an office block on Endell Street. It was overlooked by several floors of conference rooms and offices, so, again, wasn't exactly the most private spot in London. But Bob felt comfortable there and always managed to squeeze himself into the shrubbery so that he could get on with things as quickly and efficiently as possible.

Like all cats, he's very methodical about toileting. He digs himself a decent-sized hole, places himself over it while he does the necessary, then starts scrabbling dirt to cover up the evidence. He always levels it off afterwards so that no one would know it was there. I wonder why cats do this? I read somewhere that it's a territorial thing.

The gardens in Soho Square were another favourite stop-off if we were working in that area. Dogs were banned, which meant I could relax a little more if I let Bob off the leash too. Bob was fascinated by birds and Soho Square park was filled with them. He would sit there, wide-eyed, staring at them, making a curious little noise.

Raa, raa, raa.

It sounded really cute, although it was probably quite sinister. Scientists think cats mimic eating when they see potential prey. In other words, they are practising chomping them to bits in their mouth when they catch them!

Bob loves nothing more than chasing mice and rats and other creatures when I let him loose in parks. One day, I was reading a comic book in Soho Square when he arrived with part of a rat's head dangling from his mouth.

'Bob, that's going to make you really sick,' I said.

I don't think he had any intention of eating it. Instead he took it into a corner and started playing with it. Ninety-nine times out of a hundred Bob draws admiring glances from passers-by. On that particular occasion, a few people looked at him in utter horror.

I had never been one of those cat owners who saw their pets as little angels. Far from it. Like all members of his species, Bob is a highly effective predator. If we had been living in other parts of the world, I'd have been more concerned. In parts of the USA, Australia and New Zealand, they have tried to ban cats being allowed out after dark. They claim domestic cats are doing so much damage that birdlife in particular is being endangered. This wasn't such a problem in London. As far as I was concerned, Bob was free to do what came naturally to him, as long as he didn't risk hurting or harming himself.

Apart from anything else, it is great entertainment, for him – and for me.

One day, for instance, we were looking after Titch's dog Princess again. I decided to take Bob and Princess to a small park near the flats where I live.

I was sitting on a bench with Bob on the extra-long lead I'd made for him when he suddenly spotted a grey squirrel.

Princess spotted it too. Soon the pair of them were bounding towards it. The squirrel, quite sensibly, scampered up the nearest tree, but Bob and Princess weren't deterred.

I watched them as they worked together, trying to work out how to flush the squirrel out of the tree.

Princess would bark every now and again to try and rattle the squirrel. Every time the squirrel appeared or made a move, the two would adjust their positions. Bob was covering one side, while Princess was covering the squirrel's other potential escape route at the back of the tree.

They carried on with this for twenty minutes before eventually giving up.

I'm sure some people must have thought that I was ever-so-slightly mad because I sat there giggling away, engrossed by every captivating minute of it.

Chapter 22
Public Enemy No. 1

Another summer was on its way and the midday sun was already blazing as Bob and I settled down in a shady spot outside Angel tube station. I had just got out a bowl and filled it with some water for Bob when I saw two men approaching.

'Hello there, sir. We're police officers, and members of the Community

Safety Unit for Islington. Can you tell me your name?' the older of them asked me.

'Erm, it's James Bowen. Why?'

'Mr Bowen, I'm afraid we have had an allegation of assault made against you. We are going to have to ask you to accompany us to the police station to answer a few questions,' the younger guy said. 'It shouldn't take us more than a few minutes.'

I was surprised at how calm I was. In the past I'd have started panicking. It was a measure of how much more controlled and together I was these days, since having Bob. Besides, I hadn't done anything wrong; I was just helping them with their enquiries.

My mind was churning as we walked to the police station, trying to work out who might have made this 'allegation'. I had a few thoughts already.

The most obvious explanation was that someone was just trying to muck up my day. Sadly, it was pretty common. Sometimes someone selling *The Big Issue* would do it simply to get the person away from their pitch and then claim it for themselves. I'd made the Angel tube pitch a success, and I knew several people would love to have taken it over. It wasn't nice, but it was a fact of life.

The other possibility was that someone was trying to undermine my book. By now pretty much everyone in *The Big Issue* community knew about it. More newspapers had picked up on the story and several vendors had made comments, positive and negative.

Some vendors thought that I shouldn't

be allowed to sell the magazine any more. Stupidly, I'd imagined that I was doing something positive for the magazine. Instead, it felt like I'd turned into every vendor's Public Enemy No. 1.

By the time we got to the station, both of the police officers were on first name terms with Bob. They seemed really smitten with him.

'Right, let's get Bob settled before we take you into the custody suite,' the older officer said.

We were soon joined by a blonde, uniformed female PC in her late twenties. Bob seemed to take an instant shine to her and was soon rubbing his face on her hand, purring away as he did so.

'Do you think he'd mind if I picked him up?' she said.

'Go for it,' I said, sensing that he was already at ease with her.

As I suspected, he let her scoop him up.

'Why don't you come with me, Bob, and we can see if we can sort you out with something nice to eat or drink?' she said.

I watched as she took Bob behind the main reception desk to an office area with desks and photocopiers and fax machines. Bob was fascinated by all the red lights and buzzing machines and was happy in there. So I left him there as I headed off with the officers.

'Don't worry, he's safe with Gillian,' the younger officer said to me as we went through a set of doors into the custody suite. I felt certain he was telling the truth.

I walked into an interview room with the police officer, who sat me down and asked me some questions.

'Were you near this address in Islington yesterday?'

'I'd like to help you, but I honestly don't know what you are talking about,' I said.

After about ten minutes, or less, we were done.

'OK, Mr Bowen, we'll need you to stay here for a bit while we look into this further,' the younger officer said.

I was impatient to be reunited with Bob and to get back to work though. When a duty PC offered me a cup of tea in the interview room, I asked about Bob.

'It's OK, he's with Gillian still downstairs,' he said. 'He's a pretty happy chappie down there.'

Eventually, the two officers came back into the interview room.

'I'm afraid I think we've wasted your time and our time,' they said. 'The person who made this accusation on the phone hasn't been willing to come down to give a formal statement. So there's no evidence against you and so there will be no charges.'

I was both relieved and angry. But there was no point in complaining, especially as everyone had been so decent. My main concern once more was Bob. What had they done with him for all this time?

I had to go down to the reception area to sign out. Bob was there with Gillian, looking as content as when I'd left him. But the moment he saw me his tail started swishing and his ears perked up. He leaped into my arms.

'Gosh, someone's pleased to see you,' Gillian said.

'Has he been a good boy?' I asked her.

'He's been a star. Haven't you, Bob?' she said. 'I popped out to the shops and bought him some cat milk, a pouch of meaty food and a packet of treats.'

No wonder he was so happy, I thought.

'In normal circumstances he'd have been placed with any stray dogs that were being held,' Gillian told me. 'If you'd been kept in overnight, we'd have had to think about putting him there. But luckily that won't be necessary now.'

By the time I had left the station it was getting towards sunset. All day I'd been worrying about someone stealing my pitch, so I headed back to Angel just to check. To my relief, there was no one there.

'You all right, James?' one of the flower sellers asked me.

'Yeah, just someone's idea of a joke,' I said a little bitterly. 'Reporting me for assault.'

'What's wrong with people?' he said, shaking his head in disgust.

It was a good question.

About a week later, Bob and I were selling magazines during the rush hour when an attractive, blonde lady came up to us. Bob seemed to recognise her and arched his head towards her when she kneeled down beside him.

'You don't remember me, do you?' she said to me as she made a fuss of Bob. 'Tolpuddle Street station? I was the one who looked after Bob the other week.'

'Oh, yes, of course. Sorry,' I said, genuinely mortified. 'It's Gillian, isn't it?'

'Looks like you are both doing well,' she said. 'We didn't really have much of a chance to talk when you were at the station the other day, for obvious reasons. So how did you two get together?'

She smiled and laughed out loud a couple of times as I recounted our early days together.

'Soul mates by the sound of it,' she said.

She could tell that I was busy and that the rush hour was about to begin so was soon on her way.

'I might pop by and see you again if that's all right,' she said.

'Sure,' I said.

She was true to her word and was

soon stopping by to see us regularly, often bringing gifts for Bob. He seemed to have a genuine soft spot for her.

Gillian was generous to me as well. On one occasion she brought me a coffee, a sandwich and a cookie from one of the local coffee shops. We chatted for a little while. I explained to her what was happening to us with the book and how it seemed to have generated more animosity than anything else.

'Ah, don't worry about that. People are always jealous of others' success. It sounds great,' she said. 'Your friends and family must be so proud of you.'

'Yeah, they are,' I said, giving her a sheepish smile.

The truth was that I didn't have many friends. Aside from Belle, there was no one to whom I could turn – in the good times or the bad times. I had Bob and that was about it.

It was, in part, the life that I'd made for myself. I was a product of the environment in which I'd spent the past decade. But even now that I was clean, I found it hard to establish friendships. I found it hard to trust people. The events of the past couple of weeks had underlined that. For all I knew the person who had falsely accused me could have been someone I saw every day of the week. It could have been someone I regarded as a 'friend'.

So as I looked at Bob interacting with Gillian, a part of me wished my life could be as simple and straightforward as his. He had met her in strange circumstances but had immediately sensed he could trust her. He knew that she was a decent person and so he had embraced her as a friend.

I knew it wasn't going to be easy, but I needed to take that same leap of faith. To do that, however, I had to change my life. I had to get off the streets.

Chapter 23
Pride and Prejudice

It was the first Saturday of July and the streets of central London were packed for the annual Gay Pride celebrations. The hot weather had drawn even more revellers than usual. According to the news, a million people had come out to watch the huge parade of floats filled with dancers and spectacular costumes snake its way from Oxford Circus, down Regent Street to Trafalgar Square.

I'd decided to kill two birds with one stone, and had spent the day watching the floats and fabulous outfits while also selling a few magazines at a pitch on Oxford Street near Oxford Circus tube station.

It was a valuable day for all *The Big Issue* sellers so, as a 'visitor' from Islington, I had been careful to make sure I stayed within the rules. I was also careful not to 'float': the term used to describe selling whilst walking around the streets. I'd fallen foul of that rule in the past and didn't want to do so again.

This year the crowds for Gay Pride were packed four or five deep in places, but everyone was in an incredibly good mood, including Bob.

He'd got used to being in big crowds. There had been a time when he had a slight phobia of people in really scary outfits, but his years of walking the streets of London seemed to have eased his fears. He'd seen everything from weird, silver-painted human statues and French fire-eaters to giant dragons during Chinese New Year.

Today, there was no shortage of outrageous outfits and people blowing horns and whistles. Bob took it all in his stride. He sat on my shoulders, soaking up the party atmosphere and loving the attention he was getting from the huge crowds. Quite a few people knew him by name and asked to have their picture taken with the pair of us. One or two even said they were looking forward to reading about us in our book.

'We need to write it first,' I half joked.

As the main parade drew to an end late in the afternoon, Bob and I headed towards Soho Square, when I felt a tap on my shoulder. I turned around to see an outreach worker called Holly.

'James. You're floating,' she said.

'No, I'm not,' I protested.

'You were floating, James. I saw you,' she said, adamant. 'I'm going to have to report you.'

I decided that Holly wasn't going to spoil my day and carried on enjoying the party atmosphere.

The following Wednesday, the trouble began.

Arriving in Islington just before

midday, I went to see Rita, the co-ordinator on Islington Green, to buy new
supplies of magazines.

'Sorry, James,' she said. 'I can't sell
you any. Apparently someone saw you
floating in the West End. You know the
drill. You've got to go over to Head
Office in Vauxhall.'

It was infuriating for all sorts of reasons. First and foremost, of course, it
was a complete nonsense to say I'd been
floating. Secondly it was a real bore
having to travel over to Vauxhall. But I
knew I had to keep my pitch at Angel
going. The book was just a passing
phase; I knew I couldn't turn my back
on what was still my bread and butter.

At *The Big Issue* office, I had to sit
around for half an hour before I could
see a supervisor.

'I'm afraid you are going to have to serve a one-month suspension because an outreach worker saw you floating,' he said.

I tried to defend myself but nothing helped. So I decided to take it on the chin and accept the suspension. I signed the paperwork, handed in my tabard and ID card and headed home, upset but resigned.

'That's just the way the cookie crumbles, Bob,' I sighed. 'What's that saying? No good deed goes unpunished.'

I decided to spend the month working on the book and doing a little busking. At the end of the month, I went back to *The Big Issue* office and got my tabard and ID back. I also bought a supply of magazines to take back to Angel.

'Back to business, Bob,' I said as we

caught a bus and headed back across the Thames.

Arriving back at Angel, I emerged from the station and saw my pitch was empty. So I set up as normal and got back to work.

I'd been there for about half an hour when another vendor arrived. He was a guy I'd seen around occasionally. He was relatively new to *The Big Issue* and had a rather scruffy and bad-tempered old dog.

'What are you doing? This is my pitch,' he said.

'No, it's not,' I said, looking bemused. 'This has been my pitch for more than a year now.'

'It might have been your pitch a year ago, but it's mine now,' he said. 'Go and talk to Rita. She'll fill you in.'

'I will, mate, don't you worry about that,' I said, marching straight across the High Street towards the co-ordinator's spot on Islington Green.

It was obvious immediately that something was wrong because Rita's face crumpled when she saw me.

'Oh, hi, James,' she said, refusing to make eye contact. 'Someone in Vauxhall went over my head. They told that guy he could have the pitch full-time. There was nothing I could do.'

I was lost for words.

It may sound boastful, but I made that pitch really successful. Until I arrived, no one had wanted to work there. Everyone thought people were in too much of a hurry to slow down at that spot, that they didn't have time to talk to a vendor and buy a magazine. But, largely thanks to Bob, of course, I had established myself there. Even the outreach workers had said that the number of people who came to see us was amazing. As were sales of the magazine.

'I can't believe they've done this to me,' I said to Rita. 'Is it because I've got this book deal and they assume I don't need to sell any more? Because if it is they've got it all wrong. That's only a flash in the pan. I need to keep working long-term.'

But Rita just kept shaking her head and saying, 'I don't know,' or 'I'm sorry.'

In the end I just stormed off, with Bob on my shoulders.

I am not proud of what I did next, but I felt so cheated and badly treated that I decided to take matters into my own hands.

I headed back to the tube station and confronted the guy again.

'Here's £20 for the pitch. How's that?' I said.

He pondered it for a moment then grabbed the note, picked up his magazines and headed off with his dog in tow.

I had barely been there ten minutes when he arrived back, this time with Holly.

'James, this isn't your pitch any more,' she said.

'Yes, it is. I just paid the guy £20 to get it back,' I said.

'It doesn't work that way and you know it, James,' she said.

I couldn't understand why they were doing this to me. Had I behaved so badly? Was I that unpopular amongst *The Big Issue* fraternity? I must have been. They all seemed to have it in for me.

'So can I have my £20 back?' I said to the guy.

'No. I haven't earned anything yet,' he said.

I could see that he hadn't bought any magazines, so he couldn't have spent the £20. I lost it this time and started busking about twenty feet away. I wasn't allowed to, but I didn't care.

Holly reappeared with a police officer and another outreach worker, John, in tow.

'I'm afraid I'm going to have to ask you to move on, sir. Otherwise I will have no option but to caution you,' the PC said.

'You're going to get another suspension for this, James,' Holly said.

Enough was enough. I decided that I would end my association with *The Big Issue*. I didn't feel great about it. Selling the magazine had done wonders for me. But I just felt a deep sense of injustice.

I had probably over-reacted and lost my temper when I'd discovered my pitch had been given away. I just felt betrayed, especially because Bob and I had become unofficial ambassadors for the magazine. I'd been in the *Islington Tribune* a couple of times and the *Camden Journal*. The *Independent* had even published a piece. Each and every one of them mentioned that I was selling *The Big Issue*. It was the kind of feel-good coverage the magazine wanted. We embodied the ethos of the charity: they had helped us to help ourselves. Or at least, so I thought.

Once again, I began to wonder

whether the high profile Bob and I were winning was a double-edged sword. But I knew what I had to do.

I didn't go to Vauxhall to sign my six-month suspension. As far as I was concerned, I'd sold my last copy of the magazine. I was sick of it all, and it was bringing out the worst in me.

From now on I needed to concentrate on Bob, the book and all the things that brought out the best in me instead.

Chapter 24
The One That Saves Me

The drama at Angel left me feeling lost for a little while. Deep down I knew I'd done the right thing, but I still had my moments when I worried that I'd made a bad move.

It took me a week or so to snap out of it.

'You can't dwell on it forever,' I told myself. 'You have to move on and, in particular, you have to focus on the positives, especially the book.'

For a week or two after Garry and I handed in the manuscript, I half expected a phone call saying, 'Sorry, we've made a terrible mistake.' But that didn't happen.

'We're going to publish it next spring, in March,' they told me.

I now had a target to aim for. In the meantime I had to keep earning money, so I headed back to busking – and to Covent Garden.

I had mixed feelings about this. After a couple of years selling *The Big Issue*, it felt like a little bit of a backward step. My voice had deteriorated too. Shouting out, 'Big Issue! Big Issue!' hundreds of times a day was more demanding on my voice than singing a tuneful song. Playing the guitar again took some getting used to as well. I didn't have callouses on my fingers for a start.

But there were some positives too. I tried to focus on them.

Most significantly, it was a step towards independence. *The Big Issue* had, without question, been a force for good in my life. It had helped me find a little stability. Without them I would probably never have been asked to write a book. But I'd found it hard to abide by their rules. I wasn't very good at dealing with authority. I never had been.

So being my own person again felt good. I'd got my freedom back.

Of course, the other really positive thing was that Bob and I were better known now. Thanks to the various pieces in newspapers and on the internet, we were minor local celebrities.

From the first day busking, it was clear to me that we were now drawing bigger crowds than previously. There would be times when little semicircles of tourists and shoppers would surround us, snapping away with their cameras and kneeling down to stroke Bob. I was shocked at how many people that I didn't even recognise would smile, point and say: 'Aaaah, Bob.' Bob seemed to relish it.

One of the most requested songs I played was 'Wonderwall' by Oasis. I'd played it a hundred times, but now, each time I played those familiar chords, the lyrics hit home much harder. In particular, that line in the chorus that goes: *'Maybe you're gonna be the one that saves me'*. As I looked down at Bob, I realised it could have been written for him. There was no maybe about it. He had saved me.

Another positive about being in Covent Garden, of course, was that life was never dull. The place had a rhythm and life all of its own. The busiest time of the day was the evening rush, around 7pm, when people headed home from work and even more flooded in to visit the bars, restaurants, theatres and opera houses.

You could easily spot the kids who were out for a night's clubbing. They were all mini-skirts and towering heels, leather jackets and hair gel. The opera lovers were the best dressed, often with the men in black tie and the women in grand evening dresses with plenty of bling. The area was full of characters. As we settled back into the busking routine, we seemed to attract more than our fair share of them once more.

One afternoon, a couple of weeks into summer, I noticed an unfamiliar face on the pavement a few yards away from us.

It wasn't uncommon for other people to set up in the area, trying to earn a few quid. I didn't have any problem with that, as long as they didn't interfere with our livelihood.

This guy was dark skinned and dressed quite smartly, in a suit. He had an odd-looking basket, which he placed on the floor. I guessed he was some kind of street entertainer, but I had no idea what to expect.

I sat there watching him for a few moments, hoping he might ease the boredom of another day. I wasn't disappointed. He had soon dipped into his basket and produced a yellowish snake which he draped around his neck. I was no expert on snakes, but I'd have described it as an albino python. It was quite thick and about three feet long. He then started playing around with it, asking for donations from passers-by.

'Look, Bob, we've got a snake charmer,' I smiled as I watched the impressive-looking creature coiling its way around the guy.

It was obvious Bob didn't really understand what was happening. We were a good thirty feet away so he couldn't really see properly, he settled back into his favourite position in the shade and started his afternoon snooze.

The guy had been there for about forty minutes or so when he came over to say hello. He still had the snake draped on his neck like a large piece of jewellery.

'OK, guys, how are you today?' he said, in a strong accent that I guessed was Portuguese or possibly Brazilian.

Bob had been dozing away in the afternoon sun but perked up and took a good look at the curious visitor. I could tell his mind was hard at work, trying to work out what this creature was and whether it was a welcome presence. It didn't take him long to reach his conclusion.

As Bob tilted his head forward to take a better look, the snake decided to stick out its long, forked tongue and deliver a rather scary hiss. It was like something out of *The Jungle Book*.

Bob completely freaked.

Mrow! he yowled, and jumped up at me imploring me to stick him on my shoulders. I was pretty sure that if he hadn't had his harness on he would have bolted.

'Sorry, dude, didn't mean to scare your cat,' the guy said, realising what he'd done and sliding the snake off his shoulders. 'I'm going to move away from here and see how I get on further down the road.'

Bob spent the rest of the afternoon on edge. He was so paranoid about meeting another snake that he kept attacking the straps on my rucksack. He'd been sitting on this rucksack for years and had never had a problem. But suddenly anything that reminded him of the yellow python was treated with suspicion. He kept grabbing the straps in his teeth and flicking them in the air, as if to test whether they were alive or not.

It took Bob a few days to get over the snake. It must have been confusing for him. For all these years, he'd been the only creature that rode around the streets, draped across a man's neck. I think it completely threw him to see another creature there, especially such an alien one.

Of course it was all part of being back in the wacky world of Covent Garden.

Not everyone on the streets was so understanding though. It remained a competitive and sometimes aggressive place, full of people only looking after No. 1.

Bob and I were happily whiling away an afternoon on Neal Street when a young guy pitched up with an amplifier and a microphone. He was dressed in skater-boy clothes and was wearing a baseball cap and Nike trainers. All he had was a microphone.

I ignored him and got back to playing my own music.

I wasn't able to shut him out of my mind for long though. Within minutes I heard an ear-splitting, repetitive noise booming out. He was strutting around with his mic against his lips, beat-boxing. I'm a fan of most forms of music but this really wasn't my cup of tea. As far as I was concerned it was just noise.

Bob made his opinion of this 'music' plain immediately. He cast his eyes down the street with complete disdain. Then he stood up, tilted his head at me and let me know in no uncertain terms that we should move.

I gathered my stuff and moved about seventy yards down the street where I began playing again. I could still hear the din from the young kid, but at least I could hear myself think.

Others must have complained because within half an hour or so a police van arrived. I saw the boy waving his arms around in protest at the police officers, but it didn't get him anywhere. After a couple of minutes I saw him disconnect his microphone and start to pack up.

You could almost hear the sighs of relief that must have been breathed in the offices, cafés and restaurants.

'Thank goodness that's over, eh, Bob?' I said.

My joy was short-lived.

'You're not licensed to play here, mate,' one of the police officers said, noticing me and Bob sitting there.

I decided not to push it. Easing myself

back into life in Covent Garden was difficult enough without aggravating the police. *Choose your battles, James,* I told myself. Wisely, as it turned out.

Chapter 25
An Inspector Calls

It was just after midday on Neal Street in Covent Garden and the crowds of tourists and shoppers were beginning to thicken. I'd barely got myself set up and started playing when I saw a lady in a ribbed blue jumper and trousers walking towards me. I could tell she was not a tourist. As she drew close, I saw that her jumper had epaulettes and badges and had a familiar logo on it. She was from the RSPCA: the Royal Society for the Prevention of Cruelty to Animals.

The RSPCA do a great job in preventing animal cruelty and promoting animal welfare, and had been a huge help to me and Bob in the past. Today, I got the distinct impression that their presence wasn't going to be good news.

'Hello, James, how are you today?' the lady said, producing a card with her ID on it. It showed that she was an inspector.

I was a bit thrown by the fact that she knew my name.

'Fine, thanks. What's the problem?'

'I've been asked to come and see you because I'm afraid we have had complaints that you are mistreating your cat, Bob, isn't it?' she said.

I was horrified. Who had complained? And what had they said I was doing to Bob? I felt physically sick for a moment, but knew I had to keep my wits about me in case this got serious.

'I'm sure they are unfounded allegations. I can see that you treat Bob well,' she said, giving him a little tickle under the chin. 'But I do need to have a chat with you and then examine him to make sure there's nothing wrong.'

It wasn't the first time people had accused me of mistreating Bob, of course. The complaints generally fell into three categories. The first was that I was exploiting him for my own benefit. My answer to that argument was always the same: a cat is never, ever going to do something it doesn't want to do. And it is never going to be with someone it doesn't want to be with, no matter what that person does to it. Bob was a very strong character, with a free will of his own. He wouldn't have hung around if he didn't trust and like me. And it was his choice whether he wanted to come out with me each day.

There were still days when he didn't fancy taking to the streets. They were rare, to be honest. He genuinely enjoyed being out and about, meeting people and being fussed over. But when he hid away or refused to follow me out the door I always respected his decision. There would always be those who wouldn't believe that, of course, but it was the truth.

The second common accusation was that I was mistreating him by having him on a lead. If I'd had a pound for every time I'd heard someone say, 'Oh, you shouldn't have him on a leash, he's a cat not a dog,' I'd have been a very rich man. I'd explained so many times that it was to keep him safe, I was bored at hearing myself say the words. But, again, I could keep saying it until I was blue in the face as far as some people were concerned. For them it was an open-and-shut case: I was some kind of animal-abusing monster.

The third and most upsetting allegation was that I was drugging Bob. I'd only heard that a couple of times, thankfully. It cut me to the quick both times. Given what I'd been through in the past ten years and the battle I'd fought to kick my drug habit, I found that the most hurtful insult of all.

The RSPCA inspector took out a

microchip reading device to check that Bob was microchipped, which he was, of course. The device showed up my name and address as Bob's legal owner.

'That's a good start,' she smiled. 'You'd be surprised how many cat owners don't chip their pets, even these days.'

She then checked his fur for fleas, took a look at his teeth and checked his breath, perhaps to see if there was anything wrong with his liver or maybe his kidneys. She also checked his eyes to see if they were cloudy. That made me wonder whether someone *had* tried to accuse me of drugging him. It made my blood boil to think someone would say that to the RSPCA.

I had to be positive, I told myself. I hadn't done anything wrong.

'Has Bob got any health problems that

you are aware of, James?' the inspector
asked me, her pen poised over her
notebook.

'No,' I said. 'I regularly take him to the
weekly drop-in Blue Cross clinic in
Islington. They always praise me for the
way I look after him. They've not spotted
anything so I think he's pretty healthy.'

'That's good to know, James,' she
said. 'So tell me, how did you two get
together in the first place?'

I told her the story and she nodded
and smiled throughout.

'Sounds like you were meant to be
together,' she laughed. 'He's a fine fellow,
isn't he? Don't suppose you have a
phone number that I can reach you on?'

My battered old mobile phone was
still working – just – so I gave her the
number.

'I'm happy for now,' she said, 'but I may need to follow up with another visit. Are you here every day?'

'Yeah, pretty much,' I said, already feeling uneasy.

'OK, I will give you a call or drop in to see you soon.'

She then gave Bob a final ruffle and headed off into the crowds.

On the one hand I was pleased that she had left without any major drama. But I was still worried. I knew the RSPCA had significant powers when it came to pet owners. Why was she doing a follow-up visit? What was she going to tell her superiors? What if I was prosecuted and, heaven forbid, Bob was taken away from me? I couldn't help all these things going through my head.

You're overthinking things, don't worry, I told myself.

As I headed home that evening, however, I still had a knot of anxiety in my stomach. I had an awful feeling that this was going to hang over me for a while.

About a week later the RSPCA inspector appeared again. She was a lot friendlier and more relaxed this time. Bob responded well to her as she kneeled down to check how he was doing. Again, she made some notes and asked me a couple of questions about what we'd been up to that week and what we had planned in the coming days.

Then she watched us interacting together and with the passers-by.

RSPCA inspectors are obviously trained to read animal behaviours. She could see that Bob was perfectly content to be there and to be doing his little stunts for his audience.

'I'll be in touch very soon,' she said as she left, giving Bob another friendly stroke and shaking my hand with a smile.

I carried on for an hour or so, but my heart wasn't in it. I was about to pack up when I saw the housing manager of one of the blocks of flats on Neal Street striding over. We'd clashed before over my busking. She had obviously been watching from a window and had seen the RSPCA officer shaking my hand and walking off.

'People are trying to sleep upstairs,' she said.

'It's two o'clock in the afternoon,' I said, genuinely baffled.

'Never mind that,' she said as if I was some three-year-old child. 'You shouldn't be busking here. Can't you read the sign?' And she pointed at a plaque across the road.

'But I'm not busking on that side of the road, I'm busking here,' I said. 'And I am entitled to do that if I want.'

But she obviously wasn't interested in having a debate about it.

'I've had enough of you and that cat. I'm going to call the police and have you removed,' she said, marching off.

Her argument seemed ridiculous to me. How on earth could I disturb people from their sleep in the middle of the afternoon? If anything was going to wake up her residents, it was the constant din of delivery vans and lorries and police sirens. It was crazy.

About half an hour later, I saw a police van drawing into the street a hundred yards or so away from our pitch.

'I don't like the look of that, Bob,' I said, unstrapping my guitar and packing up.

By the time two policemen had walked over, I was ready to leave.

'You have to move on,' they said.

'Yes, I know. I'm off,' I said.

The incident had really riled me. I became convinced that this lady was the one who had reported me to the RSPCA.

Back at the flat that evening, the RSPCA inspector rang me on my mobile.

'You have absolutely nothing to worry about,' she said. 'Bob's a special creature and you're doing a grand job. My advice to you is to ignore those who tell you any different.'

It was the wisest advice I'd had for a long time. And, unusually for me, I took it.

Chapter 26
Doctor Bob

I was finding it harder and harder to haul myself out of bed in the morning. For the past few weeks I'd actually grown to dread the sight of the late winter sun, leaking light through my bedroom window.

It wasn't that I didn't want to get up. I wasn't sleeping well and was usually awake by first light in any case. My reasons for wanting to hide under the duvet were very different. I knew that the moment I got up, I would just start coughing again.

I'd suffered from chest problems for some time, but recently they had got really bad. No sooner had I got up in the morning than my lungs and chest were filling up with phlegm and I was coughing really violently. At times it was so bad that I was doubling up in pain and I would begin retching and vomiting. It was awful.

I was getting really worried about it. I had tried to get rid of the coughing by dosing myself with cheap medicines from the supermarket. But it had got me nowhere.

'Take a few paracetamol and get some rest,' advised one doctor I saw. But that hadn't achieved much at all.

Bob sensed I was unwell and started paying me attention. He would wrap himself around me as if taking some kind of measurements. I'd learned the lessons of the past and didn't dismiss him this time.

'Here comes Doctor Bob,' I joked one day.

There was no question in my mind that Bob was performing some kind of diagnosis. When I was lying on the sofa or on the bed, he would often spread himself out on my chest, purring gently.

I'd read somewhere about cats having the power to heal bones with their purring. I wondered whether he was trying to somehow heal my chest. More worryingly, I wondered whether he knew something I didn't.

In a way, that was the scariest thing of

all. I knew how accurate cats could be when it comes to sniffing out illness in humans. One cat I read about, from Yorkshire, would give its owner 'strange looks' before he was about to have a fit. Famously, there was a cat called Oscar who lived in an old people's home in America and would come and sit with residents who were in their final hours. Oscar's ability to anticipate people's passing was uncanny, so much so that people dreaded seeing him sidling up to them. I hoped Bob wasn't doing something similar to me!

After a while I made another appointment at my local clinic, this time with a young doctor that a friend had recommended to me. He certainly seemed sympathetic. I told him about the coughing and the vomiting.

'I'd better take a listen to your lungs,' he said.

After checking me out with a stethoscope, he tested my breathing and chest. I'd had childhood asthma so I knew my chest was weak. He didn't say too much. He just sat there making notes. Rather too many of them for my liking.

'OK, Mr Bowen, I'd like you to have a chest X-ray,' he said. 'Take this form along to the hospital and they'll know what to do.'

There was something about his face that spooked me a little. I didn't like it.

I took the form home and stuck it on the sideboard in the front room. I then quietly forgot about it. A small part of me couldn't face the hassle. It wasn't that long ago that I'd been hospitalised with DVT. What if I had to be admitted again? What if it was something even worse? I really didn't like hospitals. I told myself that I couldn't afford to waste a day there, not earning money.

Of course, these were all excuses. The truth was that I was terrified of what an X-ray might find. It was pure stubbornness. I assumed that if I stuck my head in the sand and forgot all about it, the coughing and vomiting and all the other unpleasantness would simply go away. Of course it didn't. It only got worse.

I reached breaking point one day when I visited my book publishers. I had, at last, begun to believe that the book was finally happening. They'd mocked up a cover, with Bob sitting Zen-like on my rucksack. On the back was a picture of me, while inside was a brief note on 'the author'. I still had to pinch myself to believe it was happening.

Unfortunately, I had a coughing fit in the middle of the meeting.

'I need the toilet,' I gasped, and dashed off there.

I knew it must have looked pretty bad and that I couldn't repeat it in March. Publication was looming and I'd been told that I might be doing a few media interviews, even an appearance on television. There was also talk of book signings where I'd meet members of the public. It all seemed pretty far-fetched, but to be on the safe side I decided I had to get to the bottom of this and go for the X-ray.

I knew that, this time, I couldn't really duck out of it.

I went along to hospital and was led

into a large room. A nurse placed a big metal plate on my chest before moving behind a screen to take the X-ray.

'How did it look?' I asked the nurse, fishing for a clue.

'Fine,' she said. 'But we will send a full report to your doctor. Should be there in a few days.'

So I waited a few days then received a phone call to say I should head to my doctor's for the results. I went along with a real sense of foreboding.

I have a tendency to think the worst, as you will know by now, so I was braced to hear something terrible. I was slightly taken aback when the doctor looked at the notes attached to his copy of the X-ray images and said, 'Your lungs are completely clear, Mr Bowen.'

'Really?' I said.

'Yes. There's not a single black spot, you seem to have super healthy lungs.'

'So why am I coughing my guts up all the time?' I asked, confused.

'I suspect you've got an infection of some kind,' he said, prescribing me some heavy-duty antibiotics.

'That's it?' I said, relieved but slightly shocked to discover it was that simple.

'Well, let's see if they work,' he said. 'If not we will have to explore things a bit more.'

I was sceptical. It couldn't be that simple, I told myself. But it was. Within days my chest was feeling much better and the coughing was easing off.

My agent, Mary, had been worried about my health. She'd been anxious that the publicity and the signings that would soon be coming up might be too much for me. I knew that she had my best interests at heart.

'You seem a lot better,' she told me when we met for a chat about the publication of the book which was now just weeks away.

But it was when I got another opinion that I really knew I was in the clear.

I was lying on the bed reading a comic book. Out of nowhere, Bob appeared and jumped up. He slid up to me in the same way he had done over the previous few weeks, placing himself on my chest and purring quietly away. After a moment or two, he put his ear to my chest, doing his feline stethoscope act. He lay there for a moment, listening intently. And then, as quickly as he'd arrived, he'd gone. He just picked himself up and hopped off the bed in the direction of his favourite radiator. I couldn't help smiling.

'Thanks, Doctor Bob,' I said.

Chapter 27
A Famous Face

There is a saying that March comes in like a lion and goes out like a lamb. They were right about the first bit. There were days when the wind blowing down the alleyways of Soho and the West End made such a raw, rasping noise it could almost have been a lion's roar. Some days I struggled to feel the tips of my fingers as I played my guitar.

Fortunately, Bob was better insulated than me.

Even now, with spring around the corner, Bob still had his luxurious winter coat. His tummy was also still carrying some of the extra weight he'd put on over Christmas. The cold hardly seemed to bother him at all.

Bob and I missed Angel, but if I was honest, we were enjoying life more in Covent Garden.

We'd become a double act and seemed somehow more at home amongst the jugglers and fire-eaters, human statues and other street performers that roamed the Piazza and surrounding streets. It was a competitive place, of course, so, as we settled back into daily life in central London, we polished up our act.

Sometimes I would play my guitar

while sitting cross-legged on the pavement with him. Bob always loved that and would drape himself across the body of my guitar. We'd shake hands and he'd stand on his hind legs to collect treats. We also had a new party piece.

It had started back at the flat one day while Bob had been playing with Belle. As usual, he was tossing his shabby old Scraggedy Mouse around. Belle wanted to take it off him so that she could give it a decent wash.

'It needs a good scrubbing, Bob,' I heard her telling him. 'You can have a treat if you give it to me.'

Choosing between his Scraggedy Mouse and the treat was a real dilemma. Bob dithered for a second before going for the treat. He released the mouse from his jaws long enough to receive the little snack – and for Belle to whisk the toy from under his nose.

'Well done, Bob,' she said. 'Give me five.'

And she put her hand in the air like an American footballer or basketball player, inviting his teammates to celebrate a score.

I saw Bob raise his paw to give her an acknowledgement.

'That was cool,' I laughed. 'Bet you can't get him to do it again.'

'Bet I can,' Belle said, and did.

Since then Bob had come to associate giving a 'high five' with receiving a treat. On Neal Street it had pulled in all sorts of admirers, including some rather famous ones.

It was around 4pm on a Saturday afternoon and a couple of little girls had stopped to admire Bob. They were about nine or ten years old and were accompanied by a small group of adults, including a couple of big, burly bouncer-like guys in dark glasses. To judge by the way they were surveying the scene while the girls stroked Bob, they must have been security minders.

'Daddy, look at this,' one of the girls said excitedly.

'Oh yeah. That's a cool cat,' a voice said.

I froze to the spot. I recognised the voice immediately.

'It can't be,' I said. But it was.

Standing behind me was the unmistakeable figure of Sir Paul McCartney.

I wouldn't have expected one of the greatest figures in popular music of all time to talk to me. He was in a slightly different league to me when it came to knocking out a tune. But he seemed charming.

I had my early edition of the book alongside me on the floor and saw it catch his eye. I also had a wad of flyers advertising the first book signing the publishers had organised in three days' time.

Inside my head a little voice was saying, *Oh, go on, give him one.*

'Erm, I've written a book about me and Bob,' I told him, motioning to my ginger companion sitting at my feet. 'I'm having a signing next week if you want to come along,' I said, handing him the flyer.

To my amazement he took it.

People were flashing away with their cameras. For once it wasn't Bob they were snapping.

'We'd better move along kids,' the lady with him said. I worked out that she was his new wife, Nancy Shevell. She seemed really cool.

'Take care man and keep it going,' Sir Paul said.

I was slightly starstruck afterwards and on Cloud Nine.

There wasn't a chance of Sir Paul McCartney coming along to the signing. Why would he come? But that really didn't matter now. The book had already allowed me to achieve the impossible. I'd chatted to a member of The Beatles.

Later that afternoon, before heading home, I sat down on the pavement to give Bob a couple of treats. Tomorrow was the day of the book signing in Islington. I wanted to get an early night, although I knew I wouldn't sleep much. I also didn't want to keep Bob out for much longer as it was getting cold.

As I stroked him, I noticed immediately that his body language was very defensive. His back was arched and his body was stiff. He wasn't interested in the treats either. Instead, his eyes were fixed on something in the near distance. Something – or someone – was clearly bothering him.

I looked across the street and saw a rough-looking character staring at us.

Living your life on the streets, you develop an radar when it comes to people. I could spot a bad apple instantly and this guy looked rotten to the core. It was obvious that he was working out how to steal my money.

Bob and I had probably collected £20 in the space of half an hour. I knew better than to leave too much money on display and had slipped most of it into my rucksack. He'd obviously registered this.

I decided not to confront him. As long as he kept his distance, there was no need. Just to make sure, however, I looked across at him and nodded, as if to say: 'I've spotted you, and I know what you're thinking. So just forget about it.'

Street people speak the same language. We can convey a hundred words with a simple look or expression. He understood me immediately. He just growled, got up and slinked off.

The instant the guy disappeared around the corner, Bob relaxed.

'Don't worry, mate,' I said, slipping a little snack into his mouth. 'He's gone on his way. We won't see him again.'

Chapter 28
Cat to the Rescue!

We'd had quite a day, and had soon collected more than enough to get Bob and me a few days' worth of shopping, so I decided to head home.

Bob needed to do his business before we got the bus, so we headed for his regular spot outside the posh office block on Endell Street.

I was halfway down the street when I

felt Bob moving on my shoulders. At first I thought he was simply dying to go to the toilet.

'Hold on for another second, mate,' I said. 'We're almost there.'

But I soon realised he was just taking up a new position. Unusually, he had turned to face backwards rather than forwards.

'What's wrong, Bob?' I said, turning around.

The coast seemed clear enough to me. Bob didn't seem quite so convinced. Something was definitely bothering him.

I'd barely taken a dozen steps when all of a sudden he made the loudest noise I'd ever heard him make.

Wheeeeeow! Hssssssss!

At the same time I felt a tug on my rucksack and then an almighty scream.

Aaargh!

I swung round to see the bloke who had been staring at us earlier on Neal Street. He was bent over double with huge scratches on the back of his hand. Blood was gushing from his wounds.

It was obvious what had happened. The guy had made a lunge for my rucksack and Bob must have lashed out with his claws. He'd dug them deep into this guy's hand, ripping into the skin. Bob was still in fighting mood too. He was standing on my shoulders, snarling and hissing.

'Look what your cat's done to my hand!' the guy shouted, waving his bleeding arm at me in the gloom.

'Serves you right, you were going to mug me,' I said.

Bob was screeching and hissing at him more animatedly than ever.

Wheeeeeeoooooow! Hsssss! Hsssss!

The guy turned on his heels and stumbled off into the gloom, still holding his hand.

On the bus back home, Bob sat on my lap. He was purring steadily and had tucked his head under my arm, as he often did when he – or I – felt vulnerable. I guessed we were both feeling that way after our encounter, but I couldn't be sure, of course.

'Cats are mysterious kind of folk – there is more passing in their minds than we are aware of,' Sir Walter Scott wrote. In many ways, that was part of Bob's magic. We had been through so much together, yet he still had the ability to startle and surprise me. He'd done it again this evening.

We'd never been attacked like that.

And I'd never seen him react and defend me in that way either. I'd not been switched on to the threat this guy posed at all, but Bob had.

How had he sensed the guy was not to be trusted? And how had he detected his presence when we were walking away from Neal Street? I'd seen no sign of him anywhere. Had Bob caught a glimpse of him hiding in an alleyway? Had he smelled him?

I didn't know. I would never truly know what went on in Bob's brain. Yes, we were best friends. We had an almost telepathic bond. But that understanding didn't mean we could share our deepest thoughts. We couldn't really tell each other what we felt. As silly as it sounded, I often felt sad about that. And I did so now.

Holding him close to me as the bus lurched its way through the London traffic, I had an overwhelming urge to know what Bob had felt back there in the side street. Had he been scared? Or had he fallen back on his instincts and just dealt with it in the moment? Had he already forgotten about it, or was he thinking the same kind of thoughts as me? *I am fed up with this life. I am sick of having to look over my shoulder all the time. I want to live in a safer, gentler, happier world.*

I suspected I knew the answer. Of course he'd rather not be fighting off scumbags on the streets. Of course, he'd rather be sitting somewhere warm rather than freezing on a pavement. What creature wouldn't?

As my mind ticked over, I dipped into my pocket and pulled out a scrunched-up flyer. It was my last one. I'd given the rest away. It had a photo of me with Bob on my shoulders and read:

Come and meet
James Bowen and Bob the cat
James and Bob will be signing
copies of their new book

A STREET CAT NAMED BOB

at Waterstones,
Islington Green, London
on
Tuesday 13th March 2012 at 6pm

Bob looked at it and tilted his head. I was sure that he recognised us.

I stared at the scrap of paper for what must have been a couple of minutes, lost in my thoughts.

How many more times would I have to put myself and Bob in the firing line? Would I ever break this cycle and get us off the streets?

I flattened the flyer out neatly and folded it away in my pocket.

'I hope this is the answer, Bob,' I said. 'I really do.'

Chapter 29
Waiting for Bob

It was barely 9am but my stomach was already churning away like a cement mixer. If I felt like this now how on earth was I going to feel in nine hours' time?

Waterstones in Islington was the obvious venue for the book signing. The store was part of my story in more ways than one. Not only had the staff there helped us when Garry and I were writing the book, they even featured in one of the more dramatic scenes where I'd run in the front door, desperate and panic-stricken, when Bob had run off after being scared by an aggressive dog at Angel tube station.

In the days running up to the event, I started giving interviews to more newspapers but also for radio and television. To help me get used to this, I was sent to a specialist media trainer in central London. He taught me a few tricks of the trade. During one of the first recordings, for instance, I'd fiddled with a pen while talking. When it was played back to me, all I could hear was the sound of me tapping the pen against the desk like some manic rock drummer. It was incredibly distracting and annoying.

'People will want to know how you ended up on the streets,' the trainer told me. 'You need to be prepared for questions about how Bob helped change your life and what the future holds for you both.'

'Fine,' I said, a little nervously.

'You'll also have questions about whether you're clean of drugs,' he warned me.

'I'm happy to do that,' I said. I felt I had nothing to hide.

The signing was scheduled two days ahead of the official publication date, March 15th, which also happened to be my 33rd birthday.

I hoped that wasn't going to put a hex on everything. Birthdays hadn't been much fun for me, certainly not since my teens.

I spent my thirteenth birthday in a children's ward at the Princess Margaret Hospital for Children in Western Australia. It was a miserable time in my young life. Not long afterwards I started sniffing glue and experimenting with marijuana. It was the start of my long descent into drug addiction.

I couldn't help but look back on all my previous birthdays, what I was doing at 13 and 23, and how different my life had become.

Ten years further down the road, my life had finally taken a positive turn. When I looked back now, I found it hard to believe that I'd lived through that period. But, for good or bad, it would always be a part of me. It was certainly a part of the book. I'd decided not to sugarcoat my story, which was another one of the reasons I felt so racked with nerves.

In the hours before the signing, Bob and I were filmed by a photographer from the Reuters international news agency. He wanted to take a series of photos of us travelling around on the tube and busking on Neal Street. I was glad of the distraction.

By the time we finished, it was early evening. A damp chill was beginning to descend when we got back to Islington and made the familiar walk from Angel tube station.

There was no sign of the guy who had 'acquired' my pitch outside the tube station.

'That guy and his dog caused all sorts of trouble,' a flower seller told me when I asked about it. 'There's no one from

The Big Issue selling magazines outside Angel any more.'

'What a waste,' I said. 'I built that pitch up into a nice earner for someone.'

But that wasn't my concern any more. I had other things to worry about.

Bob and I walked through Islington Memorial Green towards Waterstones. We were early so I let Bob do his business and sat on the bench to enjoy a few quiet moments. Though I was nervous I was also really excited. A new chapter in my life was beginning.

I had so many conflicting thoughts fighting for space in my head. What if no one turned up? What if loads of people turned up and thought the book was rubbish? How would Bob react if there was a crowd? How would people react

to me? I wasn't a typical author. I was a
guy who was still operating on the
fringes of society. Or at least, that's how
it felt.

Luckily Bob was being extra cool for
both of us. He spent a couple of minutes
rooting around in a favourite little spot
then sauntered back to me. He just gave
me a look.

It's all right, mate, it's all good, he seemed
to say.

It was uncanny how he was able to
calm me.

Arriving at the bookshop about half
an hour before the signing was due to
start, there were four or five people
standing in line outside.

Ah well, someone has turned up at least, I
said to myself, relieved.

They all smiled at us and I gave them

a sheepish wave. I couldn't quite get my head round the idea that people were giving up an hour of their evening to come and meet us. There were a few more people inside the store as well. They were all stood in a queue to pay and were all holding copies of the book.

'Come upstairs to the staffroom,' said Alan, the manager. 'You can have a drink and Bob can have a saucer of milk. You can take it easy for a minute before things get under way.'

Belle, Mary, Garry and a bunch of people from the publishers were in the staffroom to wish me luck. There was also a stack of books for me to sign for general sale in the store. Someone had come up with the bright idea of having a paw-shaped stamp so that Bob could also 'sign' each book. I got to work scrawling on the first copies. Belle added the final flourishing touch with the paw stamps. There were at least two dozen books in the pile. Were they sure they'd even sell this many?

At one point a member of staff arrived, beaming.

'It's stretching all the way around the block,' she smiled.

'What is?' I said, stupidly.

'The queue. It's stretching all the way back around the corner. There's probably a hundred people there with more joining all the time.'

I was speechless. For a moment, I thought about climbing out of the open window, shimmying my way down the drainpipes and making a hasty escape!

The clock ticked down towards 6pm. Bob climbed up on my shoulders and we headed back downstairs to the shop floor. I took a sneaky look down and my heart jumped into my throat. It was heaving with people.

A table stacked with books had been laid out ready for me and Bob. The line of people was stretching along the bookshelves all the way to the entrance and out into the dark March evening. They were right. There must have been a hundred people and more in it. At the other side of the store, a separate queue of people were lined up, buying copies of the book. There was even a group of photographers and a television camera-man there.

As we started walking down the final flight of steps, the cameras began flash-ing and photographers began shouting,

'Bob, Bob, this way, Bob.'

There was even a ripple of applause and a couple of cheers.

My years on the street with Bob had taught me to expect the unexpected. But this was totally uncharted territory.

One thing was clear: we'd come too far to pass on this chance.

'Come on, Bob,' I whispered, stroking the back of his neck before taking a final, deep breath. 'No turning back now.'

Epilogue
Always

That night in March 2012 was probably the most important of my life. The book signing in Islington was a success way beyond my expectations. Paul McCartney didn't quite make it, but more than three hundred other people did. The numbers caught everyone by surprise, even the bookshop, who were cleaned out of every one of their two hundred or so copies within half an hour.

'So much for my prediction that we'd only sell half a dozen,' I joked with Alan, the store manager, after three hours of signing and interviews.

When *A Street Cat Named Bob* went on general sale two days later it became what *The Times* described as 'an instantly bestselling memoir'. It entered the bestseller list on the first weekend after publication – and remained in the UK bestseller list for the best part of a year, most of that time at No. 1.

Each Sunday, I would pick up a newspaper and look at the latest chart, shaking my head slowly. Why was it so popular? What had captured the public's imagination? After a while I gave up trying to work it out and just enjoyed it.

The book swiftly found a foreign audience too. In Italy it was *A Spasso Con Bob (A Walk with Bob)*. In Portugal it was *Minha História Com Bob (My Story with Bob)*. Whatever the language, people seemed to love the story. Most of all, of course, they simply adored Bob.

Bob and I appeared on television and radio programmes to talk about the book and its popularity. For our first major appearance on the BBC's *Breakfast* programme, I was a bundle of nerves, paranoid that Bob would be scared of the lights or the strange surroundings. But he sat happily on the sofa watching himself on the monitors in front of him. He even did a series of high fives for the hosts who seemed to be every bit as bewitched by him as everyone else. He was the star of the show.

Wherever we went I was asked the same questions. In particular, people would ask how the success of the book was changing life for the both of us.

It took a little while for the financial rewards of the book's success to trickle in, so for a few months we continued to busk on Neal Street. Gradually, however, we were able to reduce our appearances. It was such a huge relief to wake up each morning knowing we wouldn't have to face the cold and the rain. Knowing that I wouldn't have to experience that sense of uncertainty and quiet desperation that I felt when I used to set off for Angel or Covent Garden was life changing.

A small part of us would always remain there of course. We continued to make occasional appearances, but now we were doing it in order to help other people rather than ourselves.

At the beginning of 2013, for instance, we formed a relationship with the animal charity, Blue Cross. We raised almost £5,000 for them in the first week and by the end of the year had increased that to more than £20,000. It felt fantastic to be able to give something back. They were so kind to me during my early days with Bob, and continued to help us when we popped into their weekly clinics on Islington Green.

I'd often felt that Bob was my reward for some act of kindness that I'd shown someone earlier in my life. I'd felt like it was karma. By helping the Blue Cross, I felt like I was returning their generosity, performing another act of karma. I aim to do the same thing for homeless charities at some point in the future.

'Has the book made you rich?' people ask.

Well, I didn't become an overnight millionaire, but at least I knew I didn't have to scour the shelves of supermarkets for 10p tins of past-the-sell-by-date baked beans. For the first time in many years, I had a bank account and even an accountant. I had to pay taxes for the first time in more than a decade.

When you are homeless or selling *The Big Issue* you know you aren't contributing to society and that part of society resents you for that. A lot of people take great pleasure in telling you, 'Get a job, you scrounger!'

People don't always understand the general hopelessness you feel when you

are homeless, busking or even selling
The Big Issue. Paying my taxes made me
feel that I was once more 'a member' of
society. And it felt good.

There were so many other positives to
the book's success.

It improved my relationship with my
parents. The bewildered but delighted
look on my father's face when he saw the
queues at that first Waterstones signing
will live in my memory for a very, very
long time. After all the disappointments,
I felt like I'd given him something to be
proud about. At last.

Apparently he shed a tear when he
read the book back at home. He called
me up to say well done, and said the
same thing again on other occasions.
He still told me to get a haircut and a
shave, of course, but at least he stopped

nagging me to 'get a proper job'.

I also travelled to Australia again to spend time with my mother. She'd read the book and wept when reading it as well. We were able to be open and honest with each other and realised that we'd be friends from now onwards.

Another satisfying aspect of the book's success was the impact it seemed to have on people's attitude to *The Big Issue* sellers and the homeless in general. Schools and charities wrote, telling me how our story had helped them to better understand the plight of the homeless.

Bob and I were also on Facebook and Twitter. Every day it seemed we got a message from someone explaining how they no longer walked past *The Big Issue* vendors but stopped and bought a magazine. Many told me they now made a point of talking to them too. I felt a huge sense of pride in that. *The Big Issue* is a fine institution that deserves everyone's support, especially in these dark economic times.

Our story also seemed to connect with people who were facing difficult times in their lives. Some read our story of survival and drew their own strength from it. Others recognised the power animals possess to heal us humans. Again, I was immensely proud every time I received a message of this kind. I never in a million years expected that I'd touch the life of one person, let alone thousands.

A few people got a little carried away and called me and Bob 'saints'. Bob might have been a saint but I wasn't, that was for sure. You can't live a chunk of your life with the problems that I had without being damaged by your experiences. In short, Saint James of Tottenham didn't exist. He never had and he never would.

The person who did exist, however, was someone who had been given his second chance in life and was determined to seize it.

I recently received a letter from a lady in a small, rural community in Wales whose close friend had just lost her long fight against cancer. The lady had given our book to her friend during her final days. She had been so touched by it that she had, in turn, given a copy to her local Minister. During her friend's funeral in the small village chapel, the Minister had held up a copy of our book.

'This book meant a great deal to the lady at the end of her life,' he'd told the congregation. 'Bob and James are an example of the power of faith, hope and love.'

Reading this moved me to floods of tears. It was unbelievably humbling. It remained in my head for days.

Those three precious qualities – faith, hope and love – had been missing in my life for a long time. But then all three came along in the mischievous, playful, occasionally grumpy but always devoted cat who helped me turn my life around.

Bob had helped me restore my faith in myself and the world around me. He had shown me hope when I really couldn't see much of it. Most of all he had given me the unconditional love each of us needed.

During one of my television appearances on the BBC, a presenter asked me a question which threw me at first.

'What will you do when Bob is not around any more?' he asked.

I got a little emotional at the very thought of losing him, but once I'd gathered myself, I answered as honestly as I could.

'I know that animals don't live as long as us humans,' I said, 'but I will cherish every single day that I share with him. And when the time comes for him to leave, he will live on in the books that he inspired.'

They may have been the truest words I ever uttered.

The world as it was before I met Bob seemed a harsh, heartless and, yes, a hopeless place. The world I have grown to see through his eyes is very different. I am happier, healthier and more fulfilled than I have ever been. I have escaped my life on the streets. I can see a clear path ahead of me. If it had not been for the love of Bob none of this would have happened, I am sure.

I have no idea where our adventure will lead us next. But I know that, for as long as he is around, he will be at the heart of it all. He is my companion, my best friend, my teacher and my soul mate. And he will remain all of those things. Always.

Acknowledgements

Writing this book has been a collaborative process and I need to thank the team of incredibly talented and supportive people who helped me cross the finishing line. Garry Jenkins was my principal guiding hand, skilfully extracting the stories then shaping the manuscript. At Hodder, I have to thank Rowena Webb and Maddy Price along with Ciara

ACKNOWLEDGEMENTS

Foley, who edited the script. I would also like to single out the brilliant publicists Emma Knight, Kerry Hood and Emilie Ferguson. A big thanks also to Dan Williams for his superb line drawings.

At Aitken Alexander I'm totally indebted to my fantastic agent Mary Pachnos as well as the team of Sally Riley, Nishta Hurry, Liv Stones and Matilda Forbes-Watson. Thanks also to Joaquim Fernandes at Aitken Alexander and Raymond Walters and his team at R Walters & Co for their invaluable guidance and help.

Closer to home I'd like to thank my best friends Kitty and Ron for being at my side through what has been a pretty crazy year or so. It hasn't been easy at times, but they've remained steadfast and loyal and I owe them more than I can say. I'd also like to thank my mother and father for their love and support, not just in the past year but throughout the darker and more difficult earlier years when I was, I know, far from the easiest of sons.

I can't let this opportunity pass without thanking the legions of people who have written to me either directly or through social media, passing on their good wishes and sharing their experiences. I've done my best to reply to as many as possible but hope that I can be forgiven for not getting back to each and every one of you. The response has been, at times, overwhelming. Most of all, of course, I'd like to thank the little guy who remains my constant companion. I still don't know whether I found Bob or

ACKNOWLEDGEMENTS

he found me. What I do know, however,
is that without him I'd be utterly lost.

James Bowen, London, May 2013

Bob Information Page

For the latest news, stories and pictures from James and Bob, follow them on Twitter at www.twitter.com/streetcatbob, or visit their Facebook page at www.facebook.com/streetcatbob